Congressional
Research
Service

U.S.-China Military Contacts:
Issues for Congress

Shirley A. Kan
Specialist in Asian Security Affairs

June 10, 2014

Congressional Research Service

7-5700

www.crs.gov

RL32496

CRS Report for Congress

Summary

This CRS report, updated as warranted, discusses policy issues regarding military-to-military (mil-to-mil) contacts with the People's Republic of China (PRC) and provides a record of major contacts and crises since 1993. The United States suspended military contacts with China and imposed sanctions on arms sales in response to the Tiananmen Crackdown in 1989. In 1993, the Clinton Administration reengaged with the top PRC leadership, including China's military, the People's Liberation Army (PLA). Renewed military exchanges with the PLA have not regained the closeness reached in the 1980s, when U.S.-PRC strategic cooperation against the Soviet Union included U.S. arms sales to China. Improvements and deteriorations in overall bilateral relations have affected military contacts, which were close in 1997-1998 and 2000, but marred by the 1995-1996 Taiwan Strait crisis, mistaken NATO bombing of a PRC embassy in 1999, the EP-3 aircraft collision crisis in 2001, and aggressive maritime confrontations (including in 2009).

Issues for Congress include whether the Administration complies with legislation overseeing dealings with the PLA and pursues contacts with the PLA that advance a prioritized set of U.S. security interests, especially the operational safety of U.S. military personnel. Oversight legislation includes the Foreign Relations Authorization Act for FY1990-FY1991 (P.L. 101-246) and National Defense Authorization Act (NDAA) for FY2000 (P.L. 106-65). A particular issue is whether the President is required to issue waivers of sanctions. Skeptics and proponents of military exchanges with the PRC have debated whether the contacts achieve results in U.S. objectives and whether the contacts contribute to the PLA's warfighting capability that might harm U.S. and allied security interests. Some have argued about whether the value that U.S. officials place on the contacts overly extends leverage to the PLA. Some believe talks can serve U.S. interests that include conflict avoidance/crisis management; military-civilian coordination; transparency and reciprocity; tension reduction over Taiwan; weapons nonproliferation; talks on nuclear, missile, space, and/or cyber domains; counterterrorism; and POW/MIA accounting.

Policymakers could review the approach to mil-to-mil contacts, given concerns about potential crises and conflicts. U.S. officials have faced challenges in gaining cooperation from the PLA. The PLA has tried to use its suspensions of exchanges while blaming U.S.-only "obstacles" (including arms sales to Taiwan, FY2000 NDAA, and air and naval reconnaissance operations).

The PRC's harassment of U.S. surveillance ships (in 2009) and increasing assertiveness in maritime disputes showed some limits to mil-to-mil talks and PLA restraint. Still, at the Strategic and Economic Dialogue (S&ED) in July 2009, President Obama called for military contacts to diminish disputes with Beijing. The U.S. articulations in 2011-2012 of a strategic "rebalancing" to Asia (or "pivot" to the Pacific) raised an issue of how to deal with China's challenges. The Administration's "rebalance" entails not only an expansion of engagement with the PLA, but also increasing exercises. The Defense Secretary visited in September 2012 and invited the PLA Navy to participate for the first time in the U.S.-led maritime exercise, RIMPAC 2014. The PLA Navy's invited participation at RIMPAC near Hawaii in summer 2014 has raised concerns in Congress and elsewhere. The U.S. Navy has increased some "interoperability" with the PLA Navy.

The Defense Secretary issued the latest annual required report on June 5, 2014, concerning military and security developments involving the PRC, cooperation, and military-to-military contacts. Legislation in the 113th Congress includes the FY2014 NDAA (**P.L. 113-66**); FY2014 Defense Appropriations Act (**H.R. 2397**); Asia-Pacific Region Priority Act, **H.R. 4495** (Forbes); and FY2015 NDAA, **H.R. 4435** (McKeon), and **S. 2410** (Levin).

Contents

Figures

Tables

Appendixes

Contacts

Overview of and Options for Policy

U.S. leaders have applied military contacts as one tool and point of leverage in the broader policy toward the People's Republic of China (PRC). The first part of this CRS Report discusses policy issues regarding such military-to-military (mil-to-mil) contacts. The second part provides a record of such contacts since 1993, when the United States resumed exchanges after suspending them in response to the Tiananmen Crackdown in 1989. Congress has exercised important oversight.

Cooperation in the Cold War in the 1980s

Since the mid-1970s, even before the normalization of relations with Beijing, the debate over policy toward the PRC has examined how military ties might advance U.S. security interests, beginning with the imperatives of the Cold War.[1] In January 1980, Secretary of Defense Harold Brown visited China and laid the groundwork for a relationship with the PRC's military, collectively called the People's Liberation Army (PLA), intended to consist of strategic dialogue, reciprocal exchanges in functional areas, and arms sales. Furthermore, U.S. policy changed in 1981 to remove the ban on arms sales to China. Secretary of Defense Casper Weinberger visited Beijing in September 1983. In 1984, U.S. policymakers worked to advance discussions on military technological cooperation with China.[2] There were direct commercial sales to the PLA that included Sikorsky Aircraft's sale of 24 S-70C transport helicopters (an unarmed version of the Black Hawk helicopter) and General Electric's sale of five gas turbine engines for two naval destroyers.[3] Between 1985 and 1987, the United States also agreed to four programs of government-to-government foreign military sales (FMS): modernization of artillery ammunition production facilities; modernization of avionics in F-8 fighters; sale of four Mark-46 anti-submarine torpedoes; and sale of four AN/TPQ-37 artillery-locating radars.[4]

Suspensions After the Tiananmen Crackdown of 1989

The United States suspended mil-to-mil contacts and arms sales in response to the Tiananmen Crackdown in June 1989. (Although the killing of peaceful demonstrators took place beyond just Tiananmen Square in the capital of Beijing on June 4, 1989, the crackdown is commonly called the Tiananmen Crackdown in reference to the square that was the focal point of the nationwide pro-democracy movement.) Approved in February 1990, the Foreign Relations Authorization Act for FY1990-FY1991 (P.L. 101-246) enacted into law sanctions imposed on arms sales and other cooperation, while allowing for waivers in the general U.S. national interest. In April 1990, China canceled the program (called "Peace Pearl") to upgrade the avionics of the F-8 fighters.[5] In

---

[1] Michael Pillsbury, "U.S.-Chinese Military Ties?," *Foreign Policy*, Fall 1975; Leslie Gelb, "Arms Sales," *Foreign Policy*, Winter 1976-77; Michael Pillsbury, "Future Sino-American Security Ties: The View from Tokyo, Moscow, and Peking," *International Security*, Spring 1977; and Philip Taubman, "U.S. and China Forging Close Ties; Critics Fear That Pace is Too Swift," *New York Times*, December 8, 1980.

[2] Deputy Assistant Secretary of Defense for East Asian and Pacific Affairs James Kelly, "Defense Relations With the People's Republic of China," testimony at a hearing of the House Foreign Affairs Subcommittees on Asian and Pacific Affairs, and International Economic Policy and Trade on "United States-China Relations," June 5, 1984.

[3] *Wall Street Journal*, August 6, 1984, and August 2, 1985. The helicopters lacked capability to fly low and fast.

[4] Department of State and DSCA, "Congressional Presentation for Security Assistance, Fiscal Year 1992."

[5] *Jane's Defence Weekly*, May 26, 1990.

December 1992, President Bush decided to close out the four cases of suspended FMS programs, returning PRC equipment, reimbursing unused funds, and delivering sold items without support.[6]

Reengagement and Recovery from Crises

In the fall of 1993, the Clinton Administration began to reengage the PRC leadership up to the highest level and across the board, including the PLA, after suspensions over the crisis in 1989. However, results were limited and the military relationship did not regain the closeness reached in the 1980s, when the United States and China cooperated strategically against the Soviet Union and such cooperation included arms sales to the PLA. Improvements and deteriorations in overall bilateral relations affected mil-to-mil contacts, which had close ties in 1997-1998 and 2000, but were marred by the 1995-1996 Taiwan Strait Crisis, mistaken NATO bombing of the PRC embassy in Yugoslavia in 1999, and the EP-3 aircraft collision crisis in 2001.

Reevaluation

In 2001, the George W. Bush Administration continued the policy of engagement with the PRC, while the Pentagon skeptically reviewed and cautiously resumed a program of mil-to-mil exchanges. Secretary of Defense Donald Rumsfeld reviewed the mil-to-mil contacts to assess the effectiveness of the exchanges in meeting U.S. objectives of reciprocity and transparency. Soon after the review began, on April 1, 2001, a PLA Navy F-8 fighter collided with a U.S. Navy EP-3 reconnaissance plane over the South China Sea.[7] Upon surviving the collision, the EP-3's crew made an emergency landing on China's Hainan Island. The PLA detained the 24 U.S. Navy personnel for 11 days. Instead of acknowledging that the PLA had started aggressive interceptions of U.S. reconnaissance flights in December 2000 and apologizing for the accident, top PRC ruler Jiang Zemin demanded an apology and compensation from the United States. Rumsfeld limited mil-to-mil contacts after the crisis, subject to case-by-case approval, after the White House objected to a suspension of contacts with the PLA as outlined in an April 30 Defense Department memo. Rumsfeld told reporters on May 8, 2001, that he decided against visits to China by U.S. ships or aircraft and against social contacts, because "it really wasn't business as usual." Deputy Secretary of Defense Paul Wolfowitz reported to Congress on June 8, 2001, that mil-to-mil exchanges for 2001 remained under review by Secretary Rumsfeld and exchanges with the PLA would be conducted "selectively and on a case-by-case basis." The United States did not transport the damaged EP-3 out of China until July 3, 2001.

The Bush Administration hosted PRC Vice President Hu Jintao in Washington in the spring of 2002 (with an honor cordon at the Pentagon) and President Jiang Zemin in Crawford, TX, in October 2002. Afterwards, Secretary of Defense Rumsfeld, in late 2002, resumed the Defense Consultative Talks (DCT) with the PLA (first held in 1997) and, in 2003, hosted General Cao Gangchuan, a Vice Chairman of the Central Military Commission (CMC) and Defense Minister. (The CMC under the Communist Party of China (CPC) commands the PLA. The Ministry of Defense and its titles are used in contacts with foreign militaries.) General Richard Myers (USAF), Chairman of the Joint Chiefs of Staff, visited China in January 2004, as the highest ranking U.S. military officer to do so since November 2000.

---

[6] Department of State, "Presidential Decision on Military Sales to China," December 22, 1992.

[7] CRS Report RL30946, *China-U.S. Aircraft Collision Incident of April 2001: Assessments and Policy Implications*, by Shirley A. Kan et al.

Visiting Beijing in January 2004, Deputy Secretary of State Richard Armitage met with General Cao Gangchuan. Armitage acknowledged that "the military-to-military relationship had gotten off to a rocky start," but noted that the relationship had improved so that "it's come pretty much full cycle." He said that "we're getting back on track with the military-to-military relationship."[8]

Resumption

Still, mil-to-mil interactions remained "exceedingly limited," according to the Commander of the Pacific Command (PACOM), Admiral William Fallon, who visited China to advance mil-to-mil contacts in September 2005. He discussed building relationships at higher and lower ranks, cooperation in responding to natural disasters and controlling avian flu, and reducing tensions. Fallon also said that he would seek to enhance military-to-military contacts with China and invite PLA observers to U.S. military exercises, an issue of dispute in Washington.[9] In October 2005, Defense Secretary Donald Rumsfeld visited China, the first visit by a defense secretary since William Cohen's visit in 2000. After Rumsfeld's visit, which was long sought by the PLA for the perceived full resumption of the military relationship, General Guo Boxiong, a CMC Vice Chairman and the PLA's highest ranking officer visited the United States in July 2006, the first such visit since General Zhang Wannian's visit in 1998.

Reappraisal

China's rising power with greater assertiveness and aggressiveness (particularly in maritime areas), refusal to discuss nuclear weapons, cyber threats, and repeated suspensions of visits showed limitations of the results of mil-to-mil exchanges. Also, a need arose for a review of the U.S. approach of a greater stress on cooperative contacts than the PLA's antagonistic attitude and leveraging of military contacts to influence U.S. policies. The PLA has repeatedly suspended mil-to-mil contacts while blaming U.S. "obstacles" (including U.S. reconnaissance, arms sales to Taiwan, legislated restrictions on contacts with the PLA, and the Pentagon's annual report to Congress on PRC Military Power). At a news conference on March 7, 2007, Defense Secretary Robert Gates said that he did not see China as a "strategic adversary" of the United States, but "a partner in some respects" and a "competitor in other respects." Gates stressed the importance of engaging the PRC "on all facets of our relationship as a way of building mutual confidence."

Nonetheless, U.S. officials expressed concern about inadequate "transparency" from the PLA, notably when it tested an anti-satellite (ASAT) weapon in January 2007. At a news conference in China on March 23, 2007, the Chairman of the Joint Chiefs of Staff, Marine General Peter Pace, said the primary concern for the bilateral relationship is "miscalculation and misunderstanding based on misinformation." Deputy Under Secretary of Defense Richard Lawless testified to the House Armed Services Committee on June 13, 2007, that "in the absence of adequate explanation for capabilities which are growing dynamically, both in terms of pace and scope, we are put in the position of having to assume the most dangerous intent a capability offers." He noted a lack of response from the PLA to an agreement at the U.S.-PRC summit in 2006 to discuss nuclear arms.

In November 2007, despite various unresolved issues, Secretary Gates visited China, and the PLA agreed to a long-sought U.S. goal of a "hotline." Later in the month, despite a number of senior

---

[8] Department of State, "Deputy Secretary of State Richard Armitage's Media Round Table," Beijing, January 30, 2004.

[9] PACOM, William Fallon, press conference, Hong Kong, September 11, 2005; author's consultation with Pentagon.

U.S. visits to China (particularly by U.S. Navy Admirals and Secretary Gates) to promote the mil-to-mil relationship, the PRC denied port calls at Hong Kong for U.S. Navy minesweepers in distress and for the aircraft carrier USS *Kitty Hawk* for the Thanksgiving holiday and family reunions, according to the PACOM Commander and Chief of Naval Operations (CNO), Admirals Timothy Keating and Gary Roughead. The Pentagon protested to the PLA.[10] Again after the President notified Congress about arms sales to Taiwan in October 2008 and January 2010, the PLA repeated cycles of suspensions of military exchanges in what the Pentagon called "continued politicization" of such contacts. In spite of its goal of cooperative engagement, the U.S. Navy faced the PRC's dangerous harassment of U.S. surveillance ships in March and May 2009. At the U.S.-PRC Strategic and Economic Dialogue (S&ED) in July 2009 in Washington, President Obama stressed military contacts to diminish disputes with China. Later in 2009, the National Defense Authorization Act (NDAA) for FY2010 (P.L. 111-84) amended the requirement in P.L. 106-65 for the report to Congress on PRC military power to expand the focus to security developments, add cooperative elements, and fold in another requirement to report on mil-to-mil contacts, including a new strategy on such contacts. Meanwhile, Admiral Robert Willard, PACOM Commander, initiated in January 2010 reviews of approaches toward the PRC and toward Taiwan (among other concerns like North Korea) by "strategic focus groups (SFGs)."

Rebalancing

The announcements in 2011-2012 of a U.S. strategic "rebalancing" of priorities to the Asia-Pacific prompted a debate in China on how to counter what some portrayed as Cold War-like anti-China "containment" (not used by U.S. officials) and whether U.S. attention to Asia (including allies) would be sustainable given budget constraints. At the start of 2012, President Obama and Defense Secretary Leon Panetta issued new Defense Strategic Guidance on how to maintain U.S. military superiority in the face of budget cuts and to "rebalance" priorities, posture, and presence to stress attention to Asia as well as the Mideast. The Administration added adjustments to its messages about the strategy, including in National Security Advisor Tom Donilon's speeches in November 2012 and March 2013. He explained that the strategy is more a comprehensive (diplomatic, defense, and economic) "whole of government" approach than a defense-dominated initiative and that the strategy includes a constructive relationship with China (partly through expanded engagement with the PLA). The PRC Foreign Ministry welcomed those remarks. Still, the PLA's Defense White Paper of April 2013 negatively assessed that "some countries" have strengthened Asian alliances, expanded the military presence, and "frequently created" regional tensions (an apparent reference to maritime disputes in the East and South China Seas especially involving the PRC, Vietnam, Japan, and the Philippines—with the latter two being U.S. allies).

However, the Obama Administration expanded engagement with the PLA that involves exercises, a sensitive step that raised concerns about showing U.S. military technology, tactics, and techniques. Defense Secretary Panetta visited China in September 2012 and invited the PLA Navy to participate for the first time in the U.S.-led multilateral, maritime Rim of the Pacific (RIMPAC) exercise in 2014 near Hawaii. At a press conference on July 19, 2013, the Chief of Naval Operations (CNO), Admiral Jonathan Greenert, called for "interoperability" with the PLA.

---

[10] "Navy: China 'Not Helpful' on Thanksgiving," *Associated Press*, November 28, 2007; White House press briefing, November 28, 2007; *Washington Post*, November 29, 2007.

Options

In a reassessment of the U.S. strategy toward and limitations of U.S. leverage in mil-to-mil contacts to resolve disputes, policymakers have a number of options. The PRC's reduced appreciation for mil-to-mil exchanges has accompanied its rising assertiveness. Some say China's rising influence has reduced U.S. influence in relative terms. Others say U.S. power and leadership remain dominant and valued by many countries to balance against China, with the potential for the United States to shape China's rise as a responsible and law-abiding power. In this context, one option is to stay the course in urging a more mature relationship to reduce miscalculations and misperceptions, while dealing with repeated cycles in which the PLA suspends contacts and then leverages the timing when it chooses to "resume" talks. A critical view questions whether the status quo can be sustainable for long without another confrontation with China and urges stepping up substantive talks about mutual concerns and relaxing restrictions on engagement with the PLA. A critical view recognizes that over the long-term, the military relationship has remained rocky and has reflected realistically not only the antagonistic approach of the PLA but more broadly the PRC toward the United States. In this view, the crux of the challenge for the U.S. military is not misunderstanding or misperception but primarily competing (not common) interests. Alternatively, rather than either a major rise or retrenchment in reaching out to the PLA, the U.S. military could recalibrate by reducing eager requests and placing priority on the safety of U.S. military personnel in the air and at sea.

More specific options include a shift to stress multilateral settings for engagement with the PLA, so that it has to engage with many countries which can amplify their concerns. However, U.S.-PRC disputes could remain unaddressed and affect any effective cooperation in international contexts. In its first long-distance operation, the PLA Navy has cooperated with the U.S. Navy and others to fight piracy in the Gulf of Aden since December 2008. Such multilateral contact could include expanded engagement between NATO and the PLA, perhaps with close coordination between the Defense Department and allied ministries. Partly to address concerns of China's Asian-Pacific neighbors, the U.S. military could engage the PLA along with the 10-member Association of Southeast Asian Nations (ASEAN)[11] and the ASEAN Regional Forum (ARF). The International Institute for Strategic Studies has held the annual "Shangri-la Dialogue" of defense ministers in Singapore since 2002. China's absence from the forum until 2007 and refusals until 2011 to send the defense minister raised questions about China's willingness to engage with others on military matters and at an appropriately senior level.

Indeed, Defense Secretary Gates attended the Shangri-la Dialogue in June 2010 and critically declared that the United States will remain a power in the Pacific and that the South China Sea became an area of growing concern regarding the use of force, challenges to freedom of navigation, and intimidation of U.S. and other companies. Gates chastised the PLA for not following up with the top-level commitment by President Obama and Hu Jintao in 2009 to advance the mil-to-mil relationship. (Hu was the CPC General-Secretary, CMC Chairman, and PRC President.) Gates defended arms sales to Taiwan as part of U.S. policy since 1979 in part because of China's accelerating military buildup that largely has focused on Taiwan. He reiterated that his department sought sustained and reliable military contacts to reduce miscommunication, misunderstanding, and miscalculation. Such contacts would support regional security and a U.S.-PRC relationship that is positive in tone, cooperative in nature, and comprehensive in scope,

---

[11] Brunei, Burma, Cambodia, Indonesia, Laos, Malaysia, the Philippines, Singapore, Thailand, and Vietnam.

Gates emphasized.[12] (President Obama has pursued a "positive, cooperative, and comprehensive" relationship with the PRC, but the PRC has translated "positive" with a Chinese word meaning "proactive.") The PLA sent a lower-level official (PLA Deputy Chief of General Staff and Air Force General Ma Xiaotian) to the meeting and declined to host Gates for a visit in China.

By early September 2010, PRC media reported General Ma as saying positive remarks about the U.S.-PRC military relationship, but the Defense Department spokesman cautioned on September 9 that Secretary Gates was not interested in merely "engagement for the sake of engagement." Gates again visited Asia in attending in Hanoi on October 11-12 the first ASEAN Defense Ministers' Meeting Plus (ADMM-Plus) between ASEAN and its partners (Australia, China, India, Japan, Republic of Korea, New Zealand, Russia, and the United States). This time, the PLA sent a CMC Member and the Defense Minister, General Liang Guanglie, who spoke in a moderate tone even as several countries raised concerns about China's maritime claims. Further, Minister Liang invited Secretary Gates to visit in January 2011. On June 3-5, 2011, the PLA finally dispatched for the first time the Defense Minister to the Shangri-la Dialogue. Defense Secretary Gates held a meeting with General Liang Guanglie. However, the PLA did not send the Defense Minister to attend the Shangri-la Dialogue in 2012, 2013, and 2014. In Hawaii in April 2014, Defense Secretary Chuck Hagel held the first U.S.-hosted meeting with ASEAN defense ministers.

Another option is for mil-to-mil to be integrated further into the overall bilateral relationship, pursued by the Obama Administration to shape China's rise as a peaceful, responsible, and rules-based power. As Gates implied a civil-military divide, there could be useful reminders to the PLA to respect the top PRC leadership's commitment to U.S.-PRC military engagement, other aspects of PRC external policies, and international laws and norms. (Also see section below on "Civilian Control over PLA and Civil-Military Coordination.") Before Gates' visit in January 2011, Deputy Assistant Secretary of Defense Michael Schiffer said in a speech on January 6 that mil-to-mil should be a critical component of bilateral engagement. However, any setbacks to the military contacts could result in costs to the overall security, economic, and political relationship. There also could be a risk that military mistrust could drive the bilateral relationship.

At the S&ED in Washington in July 2009, President Obama stressed that increased ties between our militaries could diminish causes for disputes while providing a framework for cooperation. The Under Secretary of Defense for Policy and the PACOM Commander attended that meeting, but the PLA reluctantly sent a lower-level official. For the next S&ED in Beijing in May 2010, the Pentagon sent the Assistant Secretary of Defense for Asian and Pacific Security Affairs and the PACOM Commander, even while the PLA suspended some exchanges in claimed objection to U.S. arms sales to Taiwan. Assistant Secretary of State Kurt Campbell asserted an "innovation" to include a PLA officer (a Deputy Chief of General Staff) at the 3rd S&ED in Washington on May 9-10, 2011. Still, the Chief of General Staff planned his visit on May 15-22, days after the S&ED.

Specifically regarding the PLA's objection to U.S. arms sales to Taiwan, U.S. options include reconsidering the policy under the Taiwan Relations Act (TRA) of 1979, P.L. 96-8, to make available arms for Taiwan's self-defense. Others have called for breaking the cycles since 2008 in which Presidents Bush and Obama waited on pending arms sales to notify them to Congress all at one time, cycles that raised expectations in Beijing of changes in U.S. policy leading to escalations in Beijing's demands for compromises or negotiations. Another option would discuss with the PLA how the United States has responded to the PLA's threat posture against Taiwan.

---

[12] Secretary of Defense Robert Gates, speech at Shangri-la Hotel, Singapore, June 5, 2010.

Select Abbreviations	
AMS	Academy of Military Science
CMC	Central Military Commission
COSTIND	Commission of Science, Technology, and Industry for National Defense
CPC	Communist Party of China
DCT	Defense Consultative Talks
DPCT	Defense Policy Coordination Talks
DPMO	Defense POW/Missing Personnel Office
GAD	General Armament Department
GLD	General Logistics Department
GPD	General Political Department
GSD	General Staff Department
MR	Military Region
MMCA	Military Maritime Consultative Agreement
NDU	National Defense University
PACOM	Pacific Command
PLAAF	People's Liberation Army Air Force
PLAN	People's Liberation Army Navy

Table 1. The PLA's High Command

Central Military Commission (CMC) of the CPC			
Chairman		Xi Jinping	CPC General Secretary; PRC President
Vice Chm	General	Fan Changlong	CPC Politburo Member
Vice Chm	General, PLAAF	Xu Qiliang	CPC Politburo Member
Member	General	Chang Wanquan	Defense Minister, PRC State Councilor
Member	General	Fang Fenghui	Chief of General Staff (GSD)
Member	General	Zhang Yang	Director of GPD
Member	General	Zhao Keshi	Director of GLD
Member	General	Zhang Youxia	Director of GAD
Member	Admiral, PLAN	Wu Shengli	Commander of the Navy
Member	General, PLAAF	Ma Xiaotian	Commander of the Air Force
Member	General	Wei Fenghe	Commander of the 2nd Artillery

Notes: Jiang Zemin was installed as the previous chairman of the CPC's CMC in November 1989 and remained in this position after handing other positions as CPC General Secretary and PRC President to Hu Jintao. Jiang had ruled as the General Secretary of the CPC from June 1989 until November 2002, when he stepped down at the 16th CPC Congress in favor of Hu Jintao. Jiang concurrently represented the PRC as president from March 1993 until March 2003, when he stepped down at the 10th National People's Congress (NPC). At the 4th plenum of the 16th Central Committee in September 2004, Jiang resigned as CMC Chairman, allowing Hu to complete the transition of power. At the same time, General Xu Caihou rose from a CMC Member to a Vice Chairman, and the Commanders of the PLA Air Force, Navy, and 2nd Artillery rose to be CMC Members for the first time in the PLA's history, reflecting new appreciation and action to integrate the PLA as a joint force. Xi Jinping was named as a CMC Vice Chairman on October 18, 2010, further indicating that he would succeed Hu Jintao as the next CPC General Secretary in 2012.

In November 2012, the 7th plenum of the 17th Central Committee announced the appointments of Fan Changlong (though not a CMC Member) and Xu Qiliang to be Vice Chairmen, promoted respectively from positions as the Commanders of the Jinan MR and PLAAF. PLA officers outside of the ground forces increased from three to four on the CMC, further expanding joint representation. Contrary to Jiang Zemin, Hu Jintao transferred to Xi Jinping both positions as CPC General Secretary and CMC Chairman at the leadership transition during the 18th Party Congress, allowing Xi to consolidate the CPC General Secretary's top control over the PLA and represent the PLA on the seven-man Politburo Standing Committee. In March 2013, the 12th National People's Congress announced the new government positions of Xi Jinping as PRC President and General Chang Wanquan as Defense Minister.

The PRC Defense Minister is not equivalent to the U.S. Secretary of Defense in terms of authority or functions. The Defense Minister has no operational command of forces and primarily performs in foreign relations. The Minister oversees defense mobilization in peacetime and wartime. The Defense Minister also is a government position under the State Council (like a Cabinet) and is concurrently a State Councilor.

Table 2. Summary of Senior-Level Military Visits Since 1994

Year	Defense Secretary/Minister	Highest Ranking Officer	Defense Consultative Talks
1994	William Perry		
1995			
1996	Chi Haotian		
1997		John Shalikashvili	1st DCT
1998	William Cohen	Zhang Wannian	2nd DCT
1999			
2000	William Cohen	Henry Shelton	3rd DCT; 4th DCT
2001			
2002			5th DCT
2003	Cao Gangchuan		
2004		Richard Myers	6th DCT
2005	Donald Rumsfeld		7th DCT
2006		Guo Boxiong	8th DCT
2007	Robert Gates	Peter Pace	9th DCT
2008			
2009			10th DCT
2010			11th DCT
2011	Robert Gates	Michael Mullen	12th DCT
2012	Liang Guanglie, Leon Panetta		13th DCT
2013	Chang Wanquan	Martin Dempsey	14th DCT
2014	Chuck Hagel		

Figure 1. Map: China's Military Regions

Policy Issues for Congress

Skepticism in the United States about the value of military exchanges with China has increased with the experiences in the 1990s; crises like the PLA's missile exercises targeting Taiwan in 1995-1996, mistaken bombing of the PRC embassy in Belgrade in 1999, and the F-8/EP-3 collision crisis of 2001; and China's confrontations over maritime areas. Still, Presidents and some in Congress have striven to increase collaboration with the PLA. One long-standing issue has concerned whether travel to Asia includes visits only to China or visits also to allies.

In 2002, President George W. Bush decided to pursue a closer relationship with the PRC. As the Defense Department gradually resumed the mil-to-mil relationship in that context, policy issues for Congress included whether the Administration complied with legislation and used leverage effectively in its contacts with the PLA to advance a prioritized list of U.S. security interests, while balancing security concerns about the PLA's warfighting capabilities.

President Barack Obama met with Hu Jintao at the G-20 summit in London on April 1, 2009, and they agreed to improve the mil-to-mil relationship and set up the S&ED. The S&ED combined the Bush Administration's Strategic Economic Dialogue chaired by the Secretary of the Treasury with the Senior Dialogue chaired by the Deputy Secretary of State, used the PRC's preferred term of "strategic" instead of "senior" dialogue, and elevated the Secretary of State to a co-chair. Speaking at the 1st S&ED in Washington in July 2009, President Obama stressed military contacts to diminish disputes with China, starting the integration of military talks in the S&ED and mil-to-mil in the overall relationship. The Administration also has raised attention to a need for the PLA to coordinate with the top leaders or civilian officials.

Congressional Oversight

Congress has exercised oversight of various aspects of military exchanges with China. Issues for Congress include whether the Administration has complied with legislation overseeing dealings with the PLA and has determined a program of contacts with the PLA that advances, and does not harm, U.S. security interests. Section 902 of the Foreign Relations Authorization Act for FY1990-FY1991 (P.L. 101-246) prohibits arms sales to China, among other stipulations, in response to the Tiananmen Crackdown in 1989. Section 1201 of the National Defense Authorization Act for FY2000 (P.L. 106-65) restricts "inappropriate exposure" of the PLA to certain operational areas and requires annual reports on contacts with the PLA. Section 1211 of the National Defense Authorization Act for FY2006 (P.L. 109-163) prohibits procurement from any "Communist Chinese military company" for goods and services on the Munitions List, with exceptions for U.S. military ship or aircraft visits to the PRC, testing, and intelligence-collection; as well as waiver authority for the Secretary of Defense. The NDAA for FY2010 (P.L. 111-84) amended the requirement in P.L. 106-65 for the annual report on PRC military power to expand the focus to security developments involving the PRC, add cooperative elements, and fold in another requirement to report on mil-to-mil contacts, including a new strategy for such contacts.

One issue for Congress in examining the military relationship with the PRC is the role of Congress, including the extent of congressional oversight of the Administration's policy. Congress could, as it has in the past, consider the following options:

- Host PLA delegations on Capitol Hill or meet them at other venues

- Engage with the PLA as an aspect of visits by Codels to China

- Receive briefings by the Administration before and/or after military visits

- Hold hearings on related issues

- Investigate or oversee investigations of prisoner-of-war/missing-in-action (POW/MIA) cases (once under the specialized jurisdiction of the Senate Select Committee on POW/MIA Affairs)

- Write letters to Administration officials to express congressional concerns

- Require reports from the Pentagon, particularly in unclassified form

- Review exchanges at PACOM's Asia-Pacific Center for Security Studies (APCSS) in Hawaii

- Fund or prohibit funding for certain commissions or activities

- Pass legislation on sanctions and exchanges with the PLA

- Assess the Administration's adherence to laws on sanctions, contacts, and reporting requirements

- Obtain and review the Department of Defense (DOD)'s plan for upcoming mil-to-mil contacts, particularly proposed programs already discussed with the PLA

Foreign Relations Authorization Act for Fiscal Years 1990 and 1991

Congress has oversight of sanctions imposed after the PLA's role in the use of force in the Tiananmen Square Crackdown of 1989. Commonly called the "Tiananmen Sanctions," they were enacted in Section 902 of the Foreign Relations Authorization Act for FY1990 and FY1991 (**P.L. 101-246**). The sanctions continue to prohibit the issuance of licenses to export U.S. Munitions List (USML) defense articles and defense services to China, including helicopters and helicopter parts, as well as crime control equipment. Successive Presidents have used the waiver authority, occasionally and on a case-by-case basis. In October 2010, President Obama issued a waiver for temporary export licenses under the USML for the contingency of a landing by a civilian-operated C-130 transport plane in operations for an oil spill at sea, though it was not an export. An issue is whether President Obama is required to issue waivers and consult with Congress concerning the increased exposures of the PLA to U.S. equipment in military exchanges.

The U.S. ban on arms sales also shores up U.S. credibility and leadership, including opposition to an end to the European Union (EU)'s arms embargo against China similarly imposed for the Tiananmen Crackdown as well as in opposing Israel's certain arms transfers to the PLA. In January 2004, the EU decided to reconsider whether to lift its embargo on arms sales to China. On January 28, 2004, a State Department spokesman acknowledged that the United States held "senior-level" discussions with France and other countries in the EU about the issue of whether to lift the embargo on arms sales to China. He said, "certainly for the United States, our statutes and regulations prohibit sales of defense items to China. We believe that others should maintain their current arms embargoes as well. We believe that the U.S. and European prohibitions on arms sales are complementary, were imposed for the same reasons, specifically serious human rights abuses, and that those reasons remain valid today."[13] At a hearing of the House International Relations Committee on February 11, 2004, Representative Steve Chabot asked Secretary of State Colin Powell about the EU's reconsideration of the arms embargo against China, as supported by France. Powell responded that he raised this issue with the foreign ministers of France, Ireland, United Kingdom, and Germany, and expressed opposition to a change in the EU's policy at that time in light of the PLA's missiles arrayed against Taiwan, the referendums on sensitive political issues then planned in Taiwan, and China's human rights conditions.[14]

In the most prominent cases concerning Israel, Israeli Prime Minister Ehud Barak on July 10, 2000, responded to objections from President Clinton and Congress and told PRC ruler Jiang Zemin in a letter that Israel canceled the nearly completed sale of the Phalcon airborne early warning system to the PLA. Moreover, the PLA procured from Israel some Harpy anti-radiation drones in 2002.[15] In 2004, the United States demanded that Israel not return to China some upgraded Harpy attack drones.

---

[13] Department of State, press briefing by Richard Boucher, spokesman, January 28, 2004.

[14] See CRS Report RL32870, *European Union's Arms Embargo on China: Implications and Options for U.S. Policy*, by Kristin Archick, Richard F. Grimmett, and Shirley A. Kan.

[15] *Washington Times*, July 2, 2002; *Guangzhou Daily*, July 4, 2002; *Ha'aretz*, Tel Aviv, July 25, 2002; *Flight* (continued...)

Arms Export Control Act

In addition, the Arms Export Control Act (AECA) (**P.L. 90-629**) governs U.S. transfers of defense articles (weapons, etc.) and defense services (training, information, etc.), plus any subsequent third-party transfers without U.S. consent. Section 6 of the AECA prohibits arms sales (through letters of offer, credits, guarantees, or export licenses) governed by the act to any country that is determined by the President to be engaged in a consistent pattern of intimidation or harassment directed against individuals in the United States. The President is required to report any such determination to the House Speaker and Chairman of the Senate Foreign Relations Committee. (For example, as discussed elsewhere, in 2010, PRC diplomats harassed U.S. executives over arms sales to Taiwan, and Defense Secretary Gates objected to PRC intimidation of U.S. firms.)

In April 2013, the PRC's Defense White Paper, "Diversified Employment of China's Armed Forces," acknowledged the use of combined exercises with foreign militaries to "accelerate" the PLA's modernization. In "Military and Security Developments Involving the PRC," the Defense Secretary reported to Congress in May 2013 that PLA participation or observer status in military training exercises of nations in possession of U.S. military equipment, systems, and weapons could have unintended consequences that result in the unauthorized disclosure of defense articles, technical data, or defense services to China. The report cited the "Tiananmen Sanctions" and the AECA for denial of transfers of defense articles (including technical data) and defense services.

Joint Defense Conversion Commission (JDCC)

In China in 1994, Secretary of Defense William Perry and PLA General Ding Henggao, Director of the Commission of Science, Technology, and Industry for National Defense (COSTIND),[16] set up the U.S.-China Joint Defense Conversion Commission (JDCC). Its stated goal was to facilitate economic cooperation and technical exchanges and cooperation in the area of defense conversion.

However, on June 1, 1995, the House National Security Committee issued H.Rept. 104-131 (for the National Defense Authorization Act for FY1996) and expressed concerns that this commission led to U.S. assistance to PRC firms with direct ties to the PLA and possible subsidies to the PLA. The committee inserted a section to prohibit the use of DOD funds for activities associated with the commission. The Senate's bill had no similar language. On January 22, 1996, conferees reported in H.Rept. 104-450 that they agreed to a provision (§1343 in **P.L. 104-106**) to require the Secretary of Defense to submit semi-annual reports on the commission. They also noted that continued U.S.-PRC security dialogue "can promote stability in the region and help protect American interests and the interests of America's Asian allies." Nonetheless, they warned that Congress intends to examine whether that dialogue has produced "tangible results" in human rights, transparency in military spending and doctrine, missile and nuclear nonproliferation, and other important U.S. security interests. Then, in the National Defense Authorization Act (NDAA) for FY1997 (**P.L. 104-201**), enacted in September 23, 1996, Congress banned DOD from using any funds for any activity associated with the commission until 15 days after the first semi-annual report is received by Congress. In light of this controversy, Secretary Perry terminated the JDCC and informed Congress in a letter dated July 18, 1996. Chairman Floyd Spence of the House

---

(...continued)

International, November 5-11, 2002; and Defense Secretary's report on "PRC Military Power," submitted in July 2003.

[16] CRS Report 96-889, *China: Commission of Science, Technology, and Industry for National Defense (COSTIND) and Defense Industries*, by Shirley A. Kan.

Committee on National Security had the General Accounting Office (GAO) audit the activities of the JDCC, as reported in GAO/NSIAD-96-230R of September 30, 1996.

Past Reporting Requirement

Also in 1996, the House National Security Committee issued H.Rept. 104-563 (for the NDAA of FY1997) that sought a "full accounting and detailed presentation" of all DOD interaction with the PRC government and PLA, including technology-sharing, conducted during 1994-1996 and proposed for 1997-1998, and required a classified and unclassified report by February 1, 1997. DOD submitted the unclassified report on February 21, 1997, and did not submit a classified version, saying that the unclassified report was comprehensive and that no contacts covered in the report included the release of classified material or technology sharing.

Programs of Exchanges

Certain Members of Congress have written to the Secretary of Defense to express concerns that mil-to-mil exchanges have not adequately benefitted U.S. interests. In early 1999, under the Clinton Administration, the *Washington Times* disclosed the existence of a "Gameplan for 1999 U.S.-Sino Defense Exchanges," and Pentagon spokesperson Kenneth Bacon confirmed that an exchange program had been under way for years.[17] Representative Dana Rohrabacher wrote a letter to Secretary of Defense William Cohen, saying that "after reviewing the 'Game Plan,' it appears evident that a number of events involving PLA logistics, acquisitions, quartermaster and chemical corps representatives may benefit PLA modernization to the detriment of our allies in the Pacific region and, ultimately, the lives of own service members." He requested a detailed written description of various exchanges.[18]

In December 2001, under the Bush Administration, Senator Bob Smith and Representative Dana Rohrabacher wrote to Secretary of Defense Donald Rumsfeld, expressing concerns about renewed military contacts with the PRC. They contended that military exchanges failed to reduce tensions (evident in the EP-3 crisis), lacked reciprocity, and provided militarily-useful information to the PLA. They charged that the Clinton Administration "largely ignored" the spirit and intent of legislation governing military exchanges with the PLA, including a "violation" of the law by allowing the PLA to visit the Joint Forces Command in August 2000, and, as initiators of the legislation, they "reminded" Rumsfeld of the congressional restrictions.[19]

Restrictions in the FY2000 NDAA

Congress passed legislation concerning limits to helping the PLA's warfighting capabilities. Enacted on October 5, 1999, and based on an amendment introduced by Representative Tom DeLay, the FY2000 NDAA set parameters to contacts with the PLA. Section 1201(a) of the NDAA for FY2000 (**P.L. 106-65**) prohibits the Secretary of Defense from authorizing any mil-to-mil contact with the PLA if that contact would "create a national security risk due to an

---

[17] Bill Gertz, "Military Exchanges with Beijing Raises Security Concerns," *Washington Times*, February 19, 1999.

[18] Dana Rohrabacher, letters to William Cohen, March 1, 1999 and March 18, 1999.

[19] Bob Smith and Dana Rohrabacher, letter to Donald Rumsfeld, December 17, 2001.

inappropriate exposure" of the PLA to any of the following **12 operational areas** (with exceptions granted only to any search and rescue or humanitarian operation or exercise):

- Force projection operations

- Nuclear operations

- Advanced combined-arms and joint combat operations

- Advanced logistical operations

- Chemical and biological defense and other capabilities related to weapons of mass destruction

- Surveillance and reconnaissance operations

- Joint warfighting experiments and other activities related to transformations in warfare

- Military space operations

- Other advanced capabilities of the Armed Forces

- Arms sales or military-related technology transfers

- Release of classified or restricted information

- Access to a DOD laboratory.

Section 1201(d) of the FY2000 NDAA required the Secretary of Defense to submit an annual written certification by December 31 of each year as to whether any military contact with China that the Secretary of Defense authorized in that year was a "violation" of the restrictions in the law. Options include an alternative determination by an objective observer outside or inside the Defense Department, such as the Defense Technology Security Administration (DTSA). On May 26, 2011, the House passed H.R. 1540, the FY2012 NDAA, with Section 1071(s) to remove subsection (d) that required the certification. The final bill did not keep the section.

The PLA has objected to the U.S. law as an "obstacle" to the mil-to-mil relationship, blaming the U.S. side. Under the Bush and Obama Administrations, the Pentagon cautioned that it would not be necessary to change or lift the law to enhance exchanges, while the law contains prudent parameters that do not ban all contacts. A third option would be for Congress or the Secretary of Defense to clarify what type of mil-to-mil contact with the PLA would "create a national security risk due to an inappropriate exposure." At a hearing of the House Armed Services Committee on March 9, 2006, Admiral William Fallon, the PACOM Commander, raised with Representative Victor Snyder the issue of whether to modify this law to relax restrictions on contacts with the PLA.[20] At a hearing of the House Armed Services Committee on June 13, 2007, Deputy Under Secretary of Defense Richard Lawless contended that limitations in the law should not change. The PACOM Commander, Admiral Robert Willard, testified that he agreed with Secretary Gates that "no exchanges today approach the point where the provisions would prohibit the activity," at a hearing of the House Armed Services Committee on January 13, 2010.

---

[20] House Armed Services Committee, hearing on the FY2007 Budget for PACOM, March 9, 2006. Admiral Fallon also discussed a consideration of modifying the law in an interview: Tony Capaccio, "Fallon Wants to Jumpstart Military Contacts between U.S., China," *Bloomberg*, March 13, 2006.

RIMPAC 2014

In June 2012, the PLA questioned the visiting PACOM Commander, Admiral Samuel Locklear, about why the PLA Navy was not invited to the U.S.-led RIMPAC 2012 maritime exercise based in Hawaii. (Training at RIMPAC 2012 involved over 25,000 military personnel, primarily from the United States, its allies, and partners.) The PLA's idea seemed sensitive, partly because of U.S. laws. Moreover, at the time, the Chairman of the Joint Chiefs of Staff, General Martin Dempsey, pointed out that the PLA was not willing to participate at the annual Shangri-la meetings at the level of defense minister, like other militaries. The Pacific Fleet Commander, Admiral Cecil Haney, indicated that looking for exchanges with the PLA could include its potential invitation to a humanitarian assistance/disaster relief (HA/DR) part of a future RIMPAC. Nevertheless, by September, Defense Secretary Panetta announced at a senior level that the U.S. Navy will invite the PLAN to participate in (not just observe) RIMPAC 2014. The U.S. Navy invited the PLA Navy to join at least five warfare areas of RIMPAC 2014: drills on surface warfare (limited to surface gunnery); counter-piracy; HA/DR and military medicine; search and rescue; and dive and salvage involved in explosive ordnance disposal. From June 26 to August 1, RIMPAC 2014 is expected to include four PLAN ships (destroyer, frigate, oiler, hospital ship).

The PLAN's participation has raised some concerns in Congress and elsewhere about protecting U.S. and allied technology, tactics, techniques, and procedures; preventing disclosure of defense articles and services; complying with U.S. laws; and whether to invite Taiwan. Representatives Dana Rohrabacher and Steven Chabot raised objections. The House Armed Services Committee's report of June 7, 2013, on the House-passed FY2014 NDAA, **H.R. 1960,** included Representative Randy Forbes' amendment to require the Navy Secretary to brief Congress on the PLAN's participation in RIMPAC 2014 and compliance with laws (including the FY2000 NDAA). On July 24, the House considered an amendment to **H.R. 2397**, Defense Department Appropriations Act for FY2014, sponsored by Representative Steve Stockman to ban the use of funds for U.S. military exercises that include PLA participation (including RIMPAC). Representatives Stockman and Rohrabacher spoke in favor, and Representatives Visclosky and Frelinghuysen spoke in opposition. The amendment failed by a vote of 137-286 (10 not voting). On October 21, Representative Forbes led eight Members to send a letter to Defense Secretary Hagel, urging him to invite Taiwan's military to participate in RIMPAC 2014. On June 2, 2014, the Senate Armed Services Committee reported **S. 2410** (Levin), FY2015 NDAA, with Section 1212 to express the sense of the Senate that both the PRC and Taiwan should be afforded the opportunity to participate (not just observe) in the HA/DR parts of multilateral exercises, such as RIMPAC.

Major Legislation: Required Reports and Classification

Section 1201(f) of the NDAA for FY2000 (**P.L. 106-65**) required an unclassified report by March 31, 2000, on past military-to-military contacts with the PRC. The Office of the Secretary of Defense submitted this report in January 2001.

Section 1201(e) required an annual report, by March 31 of each year starting in 2001, from the Secretary of Defense on the Secretary's assessment of the state of mil-to-mil exchanges and contacts with the PLA, including past contacts, planned contacts, the benefits that the PLA expects to gain, the benefits that DOD expects to gain, and the role of such contacts for the larger security relationship with the PRC. The law did not specify whether the report shall be unclassified and/or classified. In the report submitted in January 2001 (on past mil-to-mil exchanges), the Pentagon stated that "as a matter of policy, all exchange activities are conducted at the unclassified level. Thus, there is no data included on the section addressing PLA access to classified data as a result of exchange activities." On June 8, 2001, Deputy Secretary of Defense Paul Wolfowitz signed and submitted an unclassified report on the mil-to-mil exchanges in 2000 under the Clinton Administration and did not provide a schedule of activities for 2001, saying that the 2001 program was under review by the Secretary of Defense.

However, concerning contacts with the PLA under the Bush Administration, Secretary of Defense Rumsfeld submitted reports on military exchanges with China in May 2002, May 2003, and May 2005 (for 2003 and 2004) that were classified "Confidential" and not made public.[21] In July 2006, Secretary Rumsfeld submitted an unclassified report on contacts in 2005.[22] Secretary of Defense Robert Gates submitted an unclassified report in June 2007 for 2006.[23] In March 2008, Deputy Defense Secretary Gordon England submitted an unclassified report to Congress for 2007.[24]

Under President Obama, Defense Secretary Gates submitted an unclassified report to Congress on March 31, 2009.[25] On June 25, 2009, the House passed H.R. 2647, NDAA for FY2010, with Section 1233 to change the requirement in Section 1202(a) of **P.L. 106-65** for an annual report (required by Congress by March 1 each year) on "PRC military power" to expand the focus to security developments involving the PRC, add cooperative elements, fold in the separate requirement to report on mil-to-mil contacts (in §1201 of P.L. 106-65), and require a new comprehensive and coordinated strategy for such contacts. On July 23, the Senate passed its version that did not include such changes to the reporting requirements. Reconciling differences, the Senate receded. On October 7, 2009, Members issued the conference report that retained the House-passed section and encouraged the Defense Secretary to examine further the implications of China's psychological, media, and legal warfare on U.S. military affairs. In this legislation, enacted as **P.L. 111-84** on October 28, 2009, Congress changed the title of the report to "Annual Report on Military and Security Developments Involving the People's Republic of China."

However, the Defense Department was late in submitting the report in 2010, 2011, 2012, 2013, and 2014, while at times citing "inter-agency coordination."[26] The Pentagon also contended that a report with the backing of the full Administration after coordination was a more authoritative U.S. report. Moreover, **P.L. 111-84** required consultation with the Secretaries of Energy and State. Still, inter-agency coordination could start earlier for the process to meet the required deadline.

---

[21] Bill Gertz and Rowan Scarborough, "Inside the Ring," *Washington Times*, May 17, 2002; author's discussions with the Defense Department and Senate Armed Services Committee.

[22] Secretary of Defense, "Report to Congress Pursuant to Section 1201(e) of the FY2000 National Defense Authorization Act (P.L. 106-65)," July 19, 2006.

[23] Secretary of Defense, "Report to Congress Pursuant to Section 1201(e) of the FY2000 National Defense Authorization Act (P.L. 106-65)," June 22, 2007.

[24] Deputy Secretary of Defense, "Report to Congress Pursuant to Section 1201(e) of the FY 2000 National Defense Authorization Act (P.L. 106-65)," March 31, 2008.

[25] Robert Gates, "Annual Report on the Current State of U.S. Military-to-Military Exchanges and Contacts with the People's Liberation Army, 2008," March 31, 2009.

[26] In some other delays related to policy toward the PRC, President Obama did not notify Congress of major pending Foreign Military Sales to Taiwan in 2009, submitting his first notifications all on one day on January 29, 2010. In September 2009, President Obama sent his advisor, Valerie Jarrett, and Under Secretary of State Maria Otero to Dharamsala, India, to talk to the Dalai Lama about putting off his visit to the White House until after the President's visit to the PRC in November 2009. President Obama met with the Dalai Lama in the White House on February 18, 2010. Into its second year, the Administration did not appoint commissioners to the Congressional-Executive Commission on China (CECC) until mid-December 2010, after an annual report of October 10, 2010.

In June 2010, the Senate Armed Services Committee reported (S.Rept. 111-201 on S. 3454) the **NDAA for FY2011** that expressed its displeasure with the Defense Department for failing to submit the annual report by the deadline of March 1. In July, five Senators wrote to Defense Secretary Gates to express "serious concern" over the "failure" of the Department of Defense (DOD) to submit the 2010 report on PRC Military Power and to ask him to submit it to Congress immediately with an explanation as to the "significant delay." They noted that the report was then almost five months overdue and that a draft report was already completed with the department several months ago. The Senators stressed that "since the responsibility for this report lies within the DoD alone, we ask for your assurance that White House political appointees at the National Security Council or other agencies have not been allowed to alter the substance of the report in an effort to avoid the prospect of angering China."[27] The Secretary submitted the unclassified report on August 16, 2010, incorporating reports on PRC military power and on military contacts.[28]

Assistant Secretary of Defense Wallace Gregson wrote to Congress on February 25, 2011, that the Pentagon needed additional time for inter-agency coordination of the annual report. On May 3, Representative Randy Forbes of the House Armed Services Committee and Congressional China Caucus wrote to Secretary Gates, expressing concern for the Defense Department's "continued disregard" of the deadline for the annual report on China and that the department failed to inform Congress with timely reports on needs and threats in the Pacific. Under Secretary of Defense for Policy Michele Flournoy responded on May 23 and cited "inter-agency coordination" for the continued delay. On August 22, Representative Forbes wrote to Defense Secretary Leon Panetta, suggesting that the continued delay was not caused by inter-agency or analytical challenges, but rather the Administration's willingness to let its compliance with laws be superseded by the diplomatic calendar with the PRC. The Secretary finally submitted the report on August 24.[29]

On May 11, 2011, at the markup of H.R. 1540, the **NDAA for FY2012**, the House Armed Services Committee adopted Representative Forbes' amendment to change the name of the report back to "Military Power of the People's Republic of China" and require information on cyber threats to the Pentagon. On May 26, the House passed H.R. 1540 with the language, but on June 22, the Senate Armed Services Committee reported S. 1253 without such language. Enacted as **P.L. 112-81** on December 31, 2011, the final legislation required reporting on cyber threats against the Defense Department but did not require the change back to the original title.

In 2012, Defense Secretary Panetta submitted the report late again, on May 17, 2012, after a visit by PRC Defense Minister Liang Guanglie on May 4-10.[30] On July 11, Chairman Howard McKeon of the House Armed Services Committee wrote to Secretary Panetta to express concerns that the annual report was submitted after the statutory deadline, was "wholly inadequate," and "minimizes the uncertainty and challenges posed by China's military build-up." He also called for the Secretary to rescind a policy of limiting the length of all reports to Congress. That day, the Defense Department issued a statement denying an intent to restrict information to Congress. The next day, a spokesman said the department rescinded the guidance to restrict the page limit on reports to Congress. The **NDAA for FY2013** (enacted as **P.L. 112-239** on January 2, 2013) required reports on the PRC's tunnel sites and nuclear weapons program; and on any critical gaps in intelligence and capabilities to counter challenges from the PRC, North Korea, and Iran. The

---

[27] John Cornyn, John McCain, James Risch, Pat Roberts, and James Inhofe, letter to Robert Gates, July 23, 2010.

[28] Secretary of Defense, "Military and Security Developments Involving the PRC 2010," August 16, 2010.

[29] Secretary of Defense, "Military and Security Developments Involving the PRC 2011," August 24, 2011.

[30] Secretary of Defense, "Military and Security Developments Involving the PRC 2012," May 17, 2012.

legislation also required additional reporting to strengthen the annual report on the PLA to include assessments of the PRC's cyber, space, nuclear, anti-access/area denial, C4ISR, and maritime law enforcement capabilities, among other information; and limit funds to no more than $7 million for the Center of Excellence on Nuclear Security in China.

Secretary of Defense Hagel submitted the annual report late in May 2013.[31] Based on S. 1197, the **FY2014 NDAA (P.L. 113-66)** requires the report to cover PLA 5th generation fighters.

In April 2014, Representatives Forbes and Hanabusa introduced **H.R. 4495**, Asia-Pacific Region Priority Act, to support the strategic "rebalance" to the region. Section 205 seeks to add to the annual report some information on developments in the PRC's maritime law enforcement capabilities. The House passed **H.R. 4435, FY2015 NDAA**, on May 22, 2014, incorporating much of the language in H.R. 4495. Section 1232 would require the annual report to include the PRC's maritime law enforcement. Section 1250 would ban the use of funds to integrate the PRC's missile defense systems into U.S. missile defense systems. (In 2013, Turkey, a NATO ally, considered a purchase of the PRC's HQ-9 system.) Section 1601 would require the Defense Secretary to report on deterring and defeating space aggression from China and Russia. On June 2, the Senate Armed Services Committee reported **S. 2410** (Levin), FY2015 NDAA, with Section 1245 to require a Presidential report on the Defense Department's strategy on maritime security in the East and South China Seas, which is to include an assessment of how U.S.-PRC military-to-military engagement might facilitate a reduction in potential miscalculation and tension. Section 1245 also would require annual briefings from the Secretary of Defense on potential U.S.-PRC military-to-military engagement and an assessment on whether they meet PACOM's objectives.

Secretary of Defense Hagel again submitted the annual report late in June 2014, after a visit by PLA Chief of General Staff Fang Fenghui in May.[32]

Prohibitions on Defense Procurement

Section 1211 of the NDAA for FY2006 (signed into law as **P.L. 109-163** on January 6, 2006) prohibits procurement from any "Communist Chinese military company" for goods and services on the Munitions List, with exceptions for U.S. military ship or aircraft visits to the PRC, testing, and intelligence-collection; as well as waiver authority for the Secretary of Defense. Original language reported by the House Armed Services Committee in H.R. 1815 on May 20, 2005, would have prohibited the Secretary from any procurement of goods or services from any such company. S. 1042 did not have similar language. During conference (H.Rept. 109-360), the Senate receded after limiting the ban to goods and services on the Munitions List; providing for exceptions for procurement in connection with U.S. military ship or aircraft visits, testing, and intelligence-collection; and authorizing waivers.

In May 2011, the House adopted an amendment to H.R. 1540, the NDAA for FY2012, proposed by Representatives Rosa DeLauro and Frank Wolf, to broaden the ban against procurement of PRC defense articles to include all entities owned or controlled by the PLA, the PRC government, or an entity affiliated with PRC defense industries. Enacted as **P.L. 112-81** on December 31, 2011, the final bill did not keep the House's broadened definition of "Communist Chinese

---

[31] Secretary of Defense, "Military and Security Developments Involving the PRC, 2013," May 6, 2013.

[32] Secretary of Defense, "Military and Security Developments Involving the PRC, 2014," June 5, 2014.

military company" but adopted the requirement (in §1243) for a report from the Defense Secretary not less than 15 days before any waiver of the ban in P.L. 109-163.

In related action, on February 18, 2011, Representative DeLauro introduced **H.Res. 106** to express the sense of the House that defense systems, including the Presidential helicopters, should not be procured from a PRC entity. On July 22, Representatives Forbes and Madeleine Bordallo led 17 Members to write to the Secretary of the Air Force to seek an explanation for the procurement of T-53A trainers from Cirrus Aircraft, which was acquired by the Aviation Industry Corporation of China (AVIC). The Senate Armed Services Committee held a hearing on November 8 on China's counterfeit electronic parts entering the U.S. defense supply chain. The Committee later issued a report on its findings in May 2012.[33]

On April 25, 2013, the House Armed Services Subcommittee on Strategic Forces held a hearing at which Representative Mike Rogers raised concerns about the Defense Department's lease of a PRC-owned commercial satellite (Apstar-7) in May 2012 for the Africa Command (AFRICOM). In May 2013, the Defense Department renewed the contract after adding new higher-level review. On June 14, the House passed the FY2014 NDAA, H.R. 1960, with Section 1605 to prohibit the Defense Secretary from contracting satellite services with a foreign entity owned by a "covered foreign country" (PRC, Democratic People's Republic of Korea (DPRK), or a state sponsor of terrorism). Section 2279 in the final legislation **(P.L. 113-66)** contains the amended prohibition. Representative Rogers explained the concern that "the military had no other option but to enter into a contract that undermined our military embargo on China and exposed our military to the risk that China may seek to turn off our 'eyes and ears' at a time of its choosing."[34]

Foreign Aid

Section 620(f)(1) of the Foreign Assistance Act of 1961 **(P.L. 87-195)** prohibits assistance to any Communist country, and specifically lists the PRC as a "Communist country" for purposes of the subsection. Section 620(h) requires the President to ensure that U.S. foreign aid is not used to promote or assist the foreign aid projects or activities of a Communist country for purposes of subsection (f). Pursuant to Section 620(f)(2), the President is authorized to remove a country from the application of Section 620(f), along with other provisions that reference it, if the President makes a determination and reports to Congress that such action is important to U.S. national interests. On December 11, 1985, acting pursuant to the authority under Section 620(f)(2), the Secretary of State removed the PRC (and Tibet) from the application of Section 620(f) for an indefinite period. Nonetheless, Section 7071(g) of the Consolidated Appropriations Act of 2010 **(P.L. 111-117)** stipulated that Section 620(h) applied to foreign aid projects or activities of the PLA, including those by any entity owned or controlled by or affiliated with the PLA. The Consolidated Appropriations Act for FY2012 **(P.L. 112-74)** repeated this ban. Section 7043(e)(2) of the FY2014 Consolidated Appropriations Act **(P.L. 113-76)** again repeated the ban.

---

[33] Senate Armed Services Committee, "Inquiry into Counterfeit Electronic Parts in the Department of Defense Supply Chain," S.Rept. 112-167, May 21, 2012.

[34] Mike Rogers, "Changing the Military's Approach to Commercial Satellite Services," *Space News*, January 13, 2014.

Leverage to Pursue U.S. Security Objectives

Objectives

At different times, under successive Administrations, DOD has pursued exchanges with the PLA to various degrees of closeness as part of the policy of engagement in the relationship with China. The record of the mil-to-mil contacts can be used to evaluate the extent to which those contacts resulted in tangible benefits to advance U.S. security goals and deterrence has been effective. Some skeptics say strategy focuses on goals, while the "relationship" is not the end in itself.

The Pentagon's last East Asia strategy report, issued by Secretary of Defense Cohen in November 1998, placed "comprehensive engagement" with China in third place among nine components of the U.S. strategy. It said that U.S.-PRC dialogue was "critical" to ensure understanding of each other's regional security interests, reduce misperceptions, increase understanding of PRC security concerns, and build confidence to "avoid military accidents and miscalculations." While calling the strategic non-targeting agreement announced at the summit in June 1998 a "symbolic" action, it asserted that the action "reassured both sides and reaffirmed our constructive relationship." The report further pointed to the presidential hotline set up in May 1998, Military Maritime Consultative Agreement (MMCA), and Defense Consultative Talks (DCT) as achievements.[35]

In March 2008, Deputy Secretary of Defense Gordon England defined these principal U.S. objectives in the annual report to Congress on contacts with the PLA:

- support the President's overall policy goals regarding China;

- prevent conflict by clearly communicating U.S. resolve to maintain peace and stability in the Asia-Pacific region;

- lower the risk of miscalculation between the two militaries;

- increase U.S. understanding of China's military capabilities and intentions;

- encourage China to adopt greater openness and transparency in its military capabilities and intentions;

- promote stable U.S.-China relations;

- increase mutual understanding between U.S. and PLA officers; and

- encourage China to play a constructive and peaceful role in the Asia-Pacific region; to act as a partner in addressing common security challenges; and to emerge as a responsible stakeholder in the world.

As discussed above on the required annual report, the NDAA for FY2010, **P.L. 111-84**, required the Defense Secretary to address the **U.S. strategy for engagement with the PLA**. In his report submitted on August 16, 2010, Secretary Gates told Congress that "sustainable and reliable" military-to-military ties are an important component of the overall U.S.-China relationship and are "necessary" for the relationship to be "comprehensive." Gates also cautioned that such military contacts are "not ends in and of themselves" and that "a sustained exchange program has been difficult to achieve." He sought to expand practical cooperation in areas in which U.S. and

---

[35] Secretary of Defense, *The United States Security Strategy for the East Asia-Pacific Region*, 1998.

PRC national interests converge and to discuss candidly those areas in which there is disagreement. He noted the challenges for the risk that "misapprehension or miscalculation" could lead to crisis or conflict. In laying out **priorities**, the Defense Department identified these:

- build cooperative capacity (based on anti-piracy operations in the Gulf of Aden),

- foster institutional understanding (particular in nuclear, space, and cyber strategies and policies), and

- develop common views (on international security like nuclear nonproliferation in North Korea and Iran, and stability in Afghanistan and Pakistan, but also "respectful discussion" of differences over China's claim to Exclusive Economic Zones (EEZs) and harassment of U.S. ships and aircraft exercising international freedom of navigation, while the United States remains "vigilant" in watching for PRC behavior that puts at risk the safety of U.S. military personnel).[36]

In August 2011, Defense Secretary Leon Panetta submitted an annual report on the PLA, which specified the mil-to-mil relationship as a critical part of the Administration's strategy to shape China's rise in a way that maximizes cooperation and mitigates risks. One policy issue concerns the effectiveness of such a strategy of shaping PRC behavior. In the annual report of June 2014, Defense Secretary Hagel asserted that mil-to-mil engagement supports U.S. objectives of promoting China's development that would be consistent with international rules and norms, and that would serve as a source of security and shared prosperity in Asia.

Debate

U.S. security objectives in mil-to-mil contacts with China have included gaining insights about the PLA's capabilities and concepts; deterrence against a PLA use of force or coercion against Taiwan or U.S. allies; reduction in tensions in the Taiwan Strait; strategic arms control; weapons nonproliferation in countries such as like North Korea, Iran, and Pakistan; closer engagement with top PRC leaders; freedom of navigation and flight; preventing dangers to U.S. military personnel operating in proximity to the PLA; minimizing misperceptions and miscalculations; and accounting for American POW/MIAs.

Skeptics of U.S.-PRC mil-to-mil contacts say they have had little value for achieving these U.S. objectives. Instead that they contend that the contacts served to inform the PLA as it builds its warfighting capability against the United States, viewed by the PLA as a potential adversary. There was concern that exchanges seemed to reward belligerence. They oppose rehabilitation of PLA officers involved in the Tiananmen Crackdown. They question whether the PLA has shown transparency and reciprocated with equivalent or substantive access, and urge greater attention to U.S. allies over China. From this perspective, the ups and downs in the military relationship reflect its use as a tool in the political relationship, in which the PRC at times had leverage over the United States. Thus, they contend, a realistic appraisal of the nature of the PLA threat would call for caution in military contacts, perhaps limiting them to exchanges such as strategic talks and senior-level talks, rather than operational areas that involve military capabilities.

---

[36] Secretary of Defense, "Annual Report to Congress: Military and Security Developments Involving the People's Republic of China 2010," August 16, 2010.

A former U.S. Army Attache in Beijing wrote in 1999 that under the Clinton Administration, military-to-military contacts allowed PLA officers "broad access" to U.S. warships, exercises, and even military manuals. He argued that "many of the military contacts between the United States and China over the years helped the PLA attain its goals [in military modernization]." He called for limiting exchanges to strategic dialogue on weapons proliferation, Taiwan, the Korean peninsula, freedom of navigation, missile defense, etc. He urged policymakers not to "improve the PLA's capability to wage war against Taiwan or U.S. friends and allies, its ability to project force, or its ability to repress the Chinese people."[37] He also testified to Congress in 2000 that the PLA conceals its capabilities in exchanges with the United States. For example, he said, the PLA invited General John Shalikashvili, Chairman of the Joint Chiefs of Staff, to see the capabilities of the 15th Airborne Army (in May 1997), but it showed him a highly scripted routine. Furthermore, the PLA allowed Secretary of Defense Cohen to visit an Air Defense Command Center (in January 1998), but it was "a hollow shell of a local headquarters; it was not the equivalent of America's National Command Center" that was shown to PRC leaders.[38]

In 2000, Randy Schriver, a former official in the Office of the Secretary of Defense, discussed lessons learned in conducting military exchanges during the Clinton Administration and argued for limiting such exchanges. Schriver assessed senior-level talks as exchanges of talking points rather than real dialogue, but nonetheless helpful. He considered the MMCA a successful confidence-building measure (before the EP-3 aircraft collision crisis less than one year later in April 2001). He also said it was positive to have PLA participation in multilateral fora and to expose younger PLA officers to American society. However, Schriver said that the United States "failed miserably" in gaining a window on the PLA's modernization, gaining neither access as expected nor reciprocity; failed to shape China's behavior while allowing China to shape the behavior of some American "ardent suitors"; and failed to deter the PLA's aggression while whetting the PLA's appetite in planning against a potential American adversary. He disclosed that the Pentagon needed to exert control over PACOM's contacts with the PLA, with the Secretary of Defense issuing a memo to set guidelines. He also called for more consultations with Congress.[39]

Warning of modest expectations for military ties and the PLA's use of "suspended" exchanges to signal messages or retaliate against a perceived wrong action, former Deputy Assistant Secretary of Defense for East Asia and the Pacific (1995-2000) Kurt Campbell contended in late 2005 that security ties can only follow, not lead, the bilateral relationship. After serving as a Deputy Assistant Secretary of State for East Asian and Pacific Affairs, Randy Schriver noted in 2007 that military engagement has continued to pursue the "same modest, limited agenda that has been in place for close to 20 years," despite a visit by Secretary of Defense Robert Gates in November 2007. In 2011, Schriver called for reducing military contacts. Later, also as former Assistant Secretary of State for East Asian and Pacific Affairs, Campbell commented in 2014 that the United States and PRC have divergent objectives in dealing with maritime incidents like the near-collision between the USS *Cowpens* and a PLA Navy ship in December 2013. U.S. goals include

---

[37] Larry Wortzel, "Why Caution is Needed in Military Contacts with China," Heritage Foundation, December 2, 1999.

[38] Larry Wortzel, Director of the Asian Studies Center at the Heritage Foundation, testimony on "China's Strategic Intentions and Goals" before the House Armed Services Committee, June 21, 2000.

[39] Randy Schriver, former Country Director for China in the Office of the Secretary of Defense during the Clinton Administration, and later Deputy Assistant Secretary of State for East Asian and Pacific Affairs during the Bush Administration, discussed military contacts with China at an event at the Heritage Foundation on July 27, 2000. See Stephen Yates, Al Santoli, Randy Schriver, and Larry Wortzel, "The Proper Scope, Purpose, and Utility of U.S. Relations with China's Military," *Heritage Lectures*, October 10, 2000.

crisis prevention, but the PRC aims to limit U.S. military operations and deployments. Moreover, the United States and PRC differ over deterrence.[40] He wrote that,

> America often employs overwhelming displays of military capability – shock and awe – to create apprehension in the minds of potential adversaries or competitors. For China, deterrence – or, perhaps better, doubt – is achieved not through overt displays of power, but through creating uncertainty in the perception of others. So, by this avenue of logic, the less operational intimacy and understanding with PLA forces, the greater the deterrent value.

Proponents of military exchanges with the PRC point out that contacts with the PLA cannot be expected to equal contacts with allies in transparency, reciprocity, and consistency. They argue that the mil-to-mil contacts nonetheless promote U.S. interests and allow the U.S. military to gain insights into the PLA, including its top leadership, that no other bilateral contacts provide. U.S. military attaches, led by the Defense Attache at the rank of brigadier general or rear admiral, have contacts at levels lower than the top PLA leaders and are subject to strict surveillance in China. In addition to chances for open intelligence collection, the military relationship can minimize miscalculations and misperceptions, and foster pro-U.S. leanings and understanding, particularly among younger officers who might lead in the future. Proponents caution against treating China as if it is already an enemy, since the United States seeks China's cooperation on international security issues. There might be benefits in cooperation in military medicine to prevent pandemics of diseases, like avian flu. During the epidemic of SARS (severe acute respiratory syndrome) in 2003, it was a PLA doctor, Dr. Jiang Yanyong, who revealed the PRC leadership's coverup of SARS cases at premier PLA hospitals.[41] Rather than bilateral exchanges, the U.S. military could engage with the PLA in multilateral venues. On October 28, 2010, the PLA hosted in Beijing the first "Pan Asian-Pacific Conference on Military Medicine." Further, since the early 1990s, Congress and the Defense Department have viewed China as the key to getting information to resolve the cases of POW/MIAs from the Korean War 1950-1953.

Citing a few examples in 1998 (the PACOM Commander's first foreign look at the 47th Group Army, a U.S. Navy ship visit to Shanghai, and naval consultative talks at Naval Base Coronado), the U.S. Naval Attache in Beijing wrote that "the process of mutual consultation, openness, and sharing of concerns and information needed to preclude future misunderstandings and to build mutual beneficial relations is taking place between the U.S. and China's armed forces, especially in the military maritime domain." He stressed that "the importance of progress in this particular area of the Sino-American relationship cannot be overestimated."[42]

Two former U.S. military attaches posted to China maintained in a report that "regardless of whether it is a high-level DOD delegation or a functional exchange of medical officers, the U.S. military does learn something about the PLA from every visit." They advocated that "the United States should fully engage China in a measured, long-term military-to-military exchange program that does not help the PLA improve its warfighting capabilities." They said, "the most effective way to ascertain developments in China's military and defense policies is to have face-to-face

---

[40] Kurt Campbell and Richard Weitz, "The Limits of U.S.-China Military Cooperation: Lessons From 1995-1999," *Washington Quarterly*, Winter 2005-2006; Randall Schriver, "The Real Value in Gates' Asia Trip," *Taipei Times*, November 16, 2007; "Bound to Fail," *Washington Times*, July 26, 2011; Kurt Campbell, "How China and America Can Keep a Pacific Peace," *Financial Times*, January 2, 2014.

[41] John Pomfret, "Doctor Says Health Ministry Lied About Disease," *Washington Post*, April 10, 2003; "Feature: A Chinese Doctor's Extraordinary April in 2003," *People's Daily*, June 13, 2003.

[42] Brad Kaplan, USN, "China and U.S.: Building Military Relations," *Asia-Pacific Defense Forum*, Summer 1999.

contact at multiple levels over an extended period of time." Thus, they argued, "even though the PLA minimizes foreign access to PLA facilities and key officials, the United States has learned, and can continue to learn, much about the PLA through its long-term relationship."[43]

Another former U.S. military attache in Beijing (from 1992 to 1995) acknowledged that he saw many PLA drills and demonstrations by "showcase" units and never any unscripted training events. Nonetheless, he noted that in August 2003, the PLA arranged for 27 military observers from the United States and other countries to be the first foreigners to observe a PLA exercise at its largest training base (which is in the Inner Mongolia region under the Beijing Military Region). He wrote that "by opening this training area and exercise to foreign observers, the Chinese military leadership obviously was attempting to send a message about its willingness to be more 'transparent' in order to 'promote friendship and mutual trust between Chinese and foreign armed forces.'"[44] However, in a second PLA exercise opened to foreign observers, the "Dragon 2004" landing exercise at the Shanwei amphibious operations training base in Guangdong province in September 2004, only seven foreign military observers from France, Germany, Britain, and Mexico attended, with no Americans (if invited).[45]

A retired admiral and PACOM Commander, Dennis Blair, co-chaired a task force on the U.S.-China relationship. Its report of April 2007 recommended a sustained high-level military strategic dialogue to complement the "Senior Dialogue" started by the Deputy Secretary of State in 2005 and the "Strategic Economic Dialogue" launched by the Secretary of the Treasury in 2006.[46] After visiting China in 2011 as Chairman of the Joint Chiefs of Staff, Admiral Michael Mullen argued for sustained dialogue in the face of disputes and potential common interests.[47]

After visiting China in 2013, the Chief of Staff of the Air Force and Commander of Pacific Air Forces wrote that "distrust and increasing misperception have made the need to improve lines of communication between our two governments and militaries all the more urgent." They argued that the two countries have "shared security interests." Moreover, they contended that, because of the growing frequency and proximity at which the U.S. and PRC militaries operate in international waters and in the airspace above the maritime domain, it is important to maintain the highest levels of safety and professionalism in military interactions and for "managing friction." The Commander of Pacific Air Forces also said he hoped to bring a C-17 to China's air show.[48]

Perspectives

Aside from a debate about how to engage with the PLA, some officials and observers warn about challenges that stem from the different perspectives between the U.S. military and PLA. A still-salient study prepared for the Defense Department's Office of Net Assessment in 1997 focused on a long-standing concern about China's misperceptions that could pose dangers to U.S. security

---

[43] Kenneth Allen and Eric McVadon, "China's Foreign Military Relations," Stimson Center, October 1999.

[44] Dennis Blasko, "Bei Jian 0308: Did Anyone Hear the Sword on the Inner Mongolian Plains?" *RUSI Chinese Military Update*, October 2003.

[45] *Xinhua*, September 2; *Liberation Army Daily*, September 3; *Jane's Defence Weekly*, September 22, 2004.

[46] Dennis Blair and Carla Hills, Task Force of the Council on Foreign Relations, "U.S.-China Relations: An Affirmative Agenda, A Responsible Course," April 10, 2007.

[47] Mike Mullen, "A Step Toward Trust with China," *New York Times*, July 25, 2011.

[48] Generals Mark Welsh and Hawk Carlisle, USAF, "Strengthening Understanding and Engagement with China's Air Force," *Air & Space Power Journal*, January-February 2014; Interview, *Defense News*, February 10, 2014.

---

interests.[49] In particular, the study focused on five "dangerous misperceptions:" (1) over-estimating U.S. hostility; (2) over-estimating U.S. weakness; (3) over-estimating U.S. decline; (4) under-estimating costs of war; and (5) under-estimating fears of neighbors to China's rising military power. As implications for U.S. contacts with the PLA, the study suggested that the Defense Department review past exchanges and plan future exchanges to rebut more directly and effectively the most dangerous misperceptions held by China's military. Nonetheless, the study cautioned that while U.S. engagement with China softened its hostility and suspicion of the United States in the 25 years after the "Shanghai Communique," it was remarkable how little China's fundamental perceptions of world politics changed. U.S. policymakers would have to consider prudently that another 25 years of "strategic dialogue" and military exchanges would not eliminate completely the PRC's dangerous misperceptions. U.S. policy might need to anticipate the persistence of such misperceptions and potential miscalculations (including China's use of force) that could surprise the United States and the failure of U.S. efforts to deter the PLA.

In 1999, the Center for Naval Analyses found in a study that U.S. and PRC approaches to military exchanges were "diametrically opposed," thus raising tension at times. While the United States has pursued a "bottom-up" effort starting with lower-level contact to work toward mutual understanding and then strategic agreement, the PRC has sought a "trickle-down" relationship in which agreement on strategic issues results in understanding and then allows for specific activities later. The study said that "the PLA leadership regards the military relationship with the U.S. as a political undertaking for strategic reasons—not a freestanding set of military initiatives conducted by military professionals for explicitly military reasons. Fundamentally, the military relationship is a vehicle to pursue strategic political ends." While recognizing that using the military relationship to enhance military modernization is extremely important to the PLA, the study contended that "it is not the key motive force driving the PLA's engagement with DOD." The report also argued that because the PLA suspects the United States uses the military relationship for deterrence, intelligence, and influence, "it seems ludicrous for them to expose their strengths and weaknesses to the world's 'sole superpower.'" It noted that using "reciprocity" as a measure of progress was "sure to lead to disappointment."[50]

In August 2011, the Defense Intelligence Officer for East Asia and a former Army Attache in Beijing wrote about multiple lessons learned that the PRC's cultural approach to relations or friendships treats them as tough business negotiations. He warned U.S. officials that "the key is to conclude all negotiations with a true win-win solution, not the promise of favor in the future."[51]

After decades of U.S. efforts to engage the PLA, including increasing "habits of cooperation," the U.S. military has continued to face challenges in mil-to-mil engagement with the PRC. Perspectives of the U.S. military and the PLA have remained critically divergent. Contrary to some expectations in the 1990s, mil-to-mil engagement has failed to deter the PRC from robust, rapid PLA modernization and what some officials have observed as assertive actions in maritime areas of dispute. Some participants in the mil-to-mil engagement have observed that the PLA has reduced the value placed on engaging with the United States, even as the PLA's modernization, roles, and interaction in the world increased. The Chairman of the Joint Chiefs of Staff, Admiral Mike Mullen, issued strategic guidance for 2011 that placed priority on U.S. security interests in

---

[49] Michael Pillsbury, "Dangerous Chinese Misperceptions: the Implications for DOD," 1997.

[50] David Finkelstein and John Unangst, "Engaging DoD: Chinese Perspectives on Military Relations with the United States," CNA Corporation, October 1999.

[51] Col. (retired) Frank Miller, "Negotiating with the Chinese," *International Affairs*, FAO Association, August 2011.

the Middle East, Afghanistan, and Pakistan. Still, he noted an increased focus on Asia-Pacific in balancing risks from an "aggressive" North Korea and a "more assertive" China and in defending international freedom of navigation. Others, however, have noted that China has been assertive in various cycles over many years. (See the **Appendix** on confrontations with the U.S. military.) Even if the PLA has not increased assertive actions, its capabilities and range have improved.

Even on relatively innocuous and cooperative efforts such as the parallel anti-piracy naval operations in the Gulf of Aden since late 2008, the PLA has not described them as useful for mil-to-mil engagement or cooperation with the U.S. Navy (at odds with U.S. goals and views). U.S. engagement with the PLA in anti-piracy included hosting the commander of the PLA Navy's task force at the Headquarters of the U.S. 5th Fleet in Bahrain in December 2010. In February 2011, Admiral Mike Mullen, Chairman of the Joint Chiefs of Staff, issued the National Military Strategy in which he stated the goals of a deeper military relationship to "expand areas of mutual interest and benefit, improve understanding, reduce misperception, and prevent miscalculation" as well as promotion of "common interests through China's cooperation in countering piracy and proliferation of WMD, and using its influence with North Korea to preserve stability on the Korean peninsula." However, on March 31, 2011, the PLA issued its 2010 Defense White Paper which included a new discussion of the PLA Navy's anti-piracy operation but did not portray this area as one for U.S.-PRC military cooperation. Indeed, the Defense White Paper did not even mention contact with the U.S. military in discussing contacts with various foreign navies. In July 2012, the commander of the PLAN's "naval escort" task force held only an "informal exchange" in Oman at the "temporary request" of the multinational Combined Task Force (CTF) 151.

At the release of that Defense White Paper, a key researcher of the PLA's Academy of Military Science (AMS), Chen Zhou, candidly highlighted a key difference between China and others. He said that unlike "Western" militaries that seek transparency as the premise for military mutual trust, the PLA saw trust as the requirement for transparency. He called for first developing common interests and respecting each other's strategic interests.[52]

Recognizing the challenges in cooperation and divergent perspectives with the PLA, the Obama Administration has tried to apply lessons learned to mil-to-mil engagement with China. While the United States has sought to build confidence in avoiding crises, the PLA has avoided giving confidence. On the eve of Secretary Gates' visit in January 2011, Deputy Assistant Secretary of Defense Michael Schiffer acknowledged some distance before achieving a deep and real "strategic understanding" between our two countries. He presented the U.S. view that mil-to-mil should be a "critical component" of the U.S.-PRC relationship; mil-to-mil should be sustained, reliable, and continuous; mil-to-mil should not be used as a "reward or favor" or "punishment or a penalty" to the United States; and mil-to-mil should not be viewed as separate from the overall bilateral relationship. The U.S. approach sought a framework to institutionalize mil-to-mil and integration of the PLA into the stated goal of "comprehensive" cooperation with China.[53]

---

[52] Interview in *Jiefangjun Bao [Liberation Army Daily]*, April 1, 2011.

[53] Author's consultations; Deputy Assistant Secretary of Defense for East Asia, "Building Greater Cooperation in the U.S.-China Military-to-Military Relationship in 2011," Institute for International Strategic Studies, Washington, DC, January 6, 2011.

U.S. Security Interests

With lessons learned, a fundamental issue in overall policy toward China is how to use U.S. leadership and leverage in pursuing a prudent program of military contacts that advances, and does not harm, a prioritized list of U.S. security interests. The Pentagon could pursue such a program with focused control by the Office of the Secretary of Defense (OSD); with consultation with Congress and public disclosures; and in coordination with allies and partners, such as Japan, South Korea, Australia, Singapore, and Taiwan. Such a program might include these objectives.

Communication, Conflict Avoidance, and Crisis Management

Confrontations and Safety

The various crises of direct confrontation between the U.S. military and PLA might call for greater cooperation with China to improve communication, conflict avoidance, and crisis management. Given confrontations in the maritime areas (particularly in 2001 and 2009), some stress that the foremost U.S. interest would be to safeguard the safety of U.S. military personnel. There are increasing concerns that options pursued thus far still leave critical challenges.

Analysts in China have studied the government's strengths and weaknesses in crisis management in light of the EP-3 crisis in 2001.[54] Nonetheless, the crisis over the EP-3 aircraft collision and subsequent confrontations have shown the limits in benefits to the United States of pursuing personal relationships with PLA leaders, the consultations under the Military Maritime Consultative Agreement (MMCA), as well as the presidential hotline. From the beginning of the crisis, PRC ruler Jiang Zemin pressed the United States with a hard-line stance, while PLA generals followed without any greater inflammatory rhetoric.[55] (See the **Appendix** for text boxes that summarize the major bilateral tensions in crises or confrontations.)

Telephones

During his second visit to China as PACOM Commander in December 1997, Admiral Prueher said that "I remember wishing I had your telephone number," in response to a PLA naval officer's question about Prueher's thinking during the Taiwan Strait crisis in 1995-1996.[56] After becoming ambassador to China in December 1999, Prueher was nonetheless frustrated when the Ministry of Foreign Affairs and the PLA would not answer the phone or return phone calls in the immediate aftermath of the EP-3 collision crisis in April 2001.[57] Personal ties were not useful in crises.[58]

---

[54] Author's discussions with government-affiliated research organizations in China in 2002.

[55] CRS Report RL30946, *China-U.S. Aircraft Collision Incident of April 2001: Assessments and Policy Implications*, by Shirley A. Kan et al.

[56] LTC Frank Miller (U.S. Army), "China Hosts Visit by the U.S. Commander in Chief, Pacific," *Asia Pacific Defense Forum*, Spring 1998. The article ended by saying that "perhaps the most important result of Adm. Prueher's December 1997 trip to China is that, should there be another crisis like the March 1996 Taiwan Strait Missile Crisis, Adm. Prueher now has the phone number."

[57] John Keefe, "Anatomy of the EP-3 Incident, April 2001," Center for Naval Analyses report, January 2002.

[58] Thomas Henderschedt and Chad Sbragia, "China's Naval Ambitions," *Armed Forces Journal*, September 2010.

Still, some continue to believe there could be benefits in fostering relationships with PLA officers, both at the senior level and with younger, future leaders. While in Beijing in January 2004, the Chairman of the Joint Chiefs of Staff, General Myers, said that "it's always an advantage to be able to pick up a telephone and talk to somebody that you know fairly well. The relationship that I have with General Liang [Chief of General Staff], the relationship that Defense Secretary Rumsfeld has with his counterpart, General Cao, is going to be helpful in that regard."[59] Likewise, visiting Beijing in September 2005, Admiral William Fallon, PACOM Commander, hoped for the value for his regional responsibilities to "pick up the telephone and call someone I already know."[60] During his visit to Beijing in July 2011, the Chairman of the Joint Chiefs of Staff, Admiral Michael Mullen, still said he wished that he could "pick up the phone" in a crisis.[61]

Maritime Disputes and Military Maritime Consultative Agreement (MMCA)

Much attention has been on the MMCA for resolving tension and preventing crisis or conflict. The MMCA, initialed at the first DCT in December 1997 and signed by Secretary Cohen in Beijing in January 1998, only arranged meetings to discuss maritime and air safety (i.e., to talk about talking). There was no agreement on communication during crises or rules of engagement. Despite the 2001 crisis, the U.S. military encountered difficulties with the PLA in discussions under the MMCA, including simply setting up meetings and PLA objections to U.S. activities in China's claimed 200-nautical mile exclusive economic zone (EEZ) (beyond the territorial sea up to 12 nautical miles from the coast).[62] In spite of the MMCA meetings since the late 1990s, the U.S. Navy and Air Force have faced challenges to operational safety and freedom of navigation. The Defense Secretary told Congress in a report in August 2010 that "the United States and China continue to have differences over the rights of coastal states in their exclusive economic zones, and the appropriate response to such differences." It also stressed that "the United States remains vigilant in its watch for behavior that puts at risk the safety of U.S. soldiers, sailors, airmen, and marines, or is in clear violation of international norms. The Department will continue to use all available channels, in particular an invigorated MMCA and Defense Policy Coordination Talks process, to communicate the U.S. government position on these and other matters to the PLA, while taking advantage of opportunities for the two sides to discuss practical ways to reduce the chances for misunderstanding and miscalculation between our armed forces."[63]

However, another assessment is that not only have dangerous confrontations occurred despite the MMCA but that the tension have been based on different national interests rather than any misperception or misunderstanding. The PLA has tried purposefully to keep U.S. military operations farther from China and restrict them even beyond the PRC's territorial seas. The Defense Secretary reported to Congress in August 2010 that his department did not observe a resurgence of harassment by PRC fishing vessels of U.S. naval auxiliary ships conducting routine and lawful military operations beyond the PRC's territorial seas that occurred in spring 2009. Still, he warned that such harassment could occur again. Moreover, two months after the Secretary's report to Congress, at a meeting of the MMCA in Honolulu in October 2010, the U.S.

---

[59] Jim Garamone, "China, U.S. Making Progress on Military Relations," *AFPS*, January 15, 2004.

[60] PACOM, Admiral William J. Fallon, "Roundtable at Embassy PAS Program Room," Beijing, September 7, 2005. Fallon also said he consulted "extensively" with retired Admiral Prueher, a former PACOM Commander.

[61] Admiral Michael Mullen, Media Roundtable, Beijing, China, July 10, 2011.

[62] Chris Johnson, "DOD Will Urge China to Conduct Joint Search and Rescue Exercise," *Inside the Navy*, March 13, 2006.

[63] Secretary of Defense, "Military and Security Developments Involving the PRC 2010," August 16, 2010.

military raised concerns to the PLA about several incidents involving unsafe and unprofessional actions by PRC ships as well as aircraft that risked the lives of U.S. sailors and airmen in the Navy and Air Force. The PLA repeated complaints about U.S. maritime and air reconnaissance by U.S. ships and planes. Critically, the PLA rejected the possibility of accidents, blaming continued U.S. operations for any risks, so that another collision would be only the United States' fault. The PLA also has limited its primary representation to the PLAN in attending MMCA meetings, while the U.S. side has interacted with the PLA at a joint level led by PACOM. In 2010, PLA fighters conducted unusually close intercepts of U.S. military aircraft operating in international airspace, in addition to harassment by PRC ships of U.S. survey ships operating outside of PRC territorial seas, reported the Secretary of Defense to Congress in August 2011. The 7th Fleet Commander said in February 2011 that the PLAN ignored ship-to-ship communication in Asia, even if it made such contact in anti-piracy operations in the Gulf of Aden (that the PLA calls "escort missions").[64]

At other times, the PLA indicated generally that it can understand the escalating dangers of accidents and collisions. In 2010, General Liang Guanglie (a CMC Member and PRC Defense Minister) acknowledged the risk of accidents. He used the phrase "an accidental discharge of gunfire in cleaning a gun" to refer to inadvertent accidents that could lead to military tension.[65]

On June 29, 2011, Taiwan's F-16 fighters flew to intercept PLA Air Force Su-27 fighters that crossed a "median line" for the Taiwan Strait to confront a U.S. reconnaissance aircraft. Then, on July 22, Secretary of State Hillary Clinton issued a statement that stressed respect for freedom of navigation as well as overflight in the South China Sea, and three days later, met with PRC State Councilor Dai Bingguo in Shenzhen and stressed freedom of navigation. In August, the two sides held an MMCA working group meeting in Qingdao and discussed disputes over the PLA's complaints against U.S. reconnaissance flights. Again, there was no MMCA plenary in 2011.

Policy issues include how to reinvigorate the MMCA talks and how to include the actions of the PLAAF and the PRC's official maritime law enforcement ships and aircraft that have coordinated with those of the PLAN and PLAAF.[66] The PLAN has shifted ships to maritime law enforcement.

---

[64] *Wall Street Journal*, February 21, 2011; and *South China Morning Post*, Hong Kong, February 22, 2011.

[65] Interview with Defense Minister Liang Guanglie published in *Renmin Ribao* [People's Daily], December 29, 2010.

[66] China's official maritime law enforcement forces included China Maritime Surveillance (CMS), under the Ministry of Land and Resources; Fisheries Law Enforcement Command (FLEC), under the Ministry of Agriculture; China Coast Guard (CCG), a paramilitary People's Armed Police (PAP) force under the Ministry of Public Security (MPS); Maritime Safety Administration (MSA) and China Rescue and Salvage (CRS), under the Ministry of Transportation; and Anti-Smuggling Maritime Police, under the General Administration of Customs. Although some analysts have attributed rising tension in China's territorial and maritime disputes to inadequate coordination among PRC agencies, there has been reported inter-agency coordination and cooperation between the PLA and the civilian maritime forces. The official ships and aircraft augment the PLA's naval ships and aircraft to assert China's claims and control. For example, On March 4-8, 2009, Y-12 maritime surveillance aircraft, a PLAN frigate, PRC patrol and intelligence collection ships, and trawlers coordinated in increasingly aggressive and dangerous harassment of unarmed U.S. ocean surveillance ships, the USNS *Victorious* and USNS *Impeccable*, during routine operations in international waters in the Yellow Sea and South China Sea. The civilian ships in involved in the "Impeccable Incident" included those from the CMS and FLEC, and the U.S. Navy special mission ships defended themselves with non-lethal force. In January 2011, Wu Shengli, CMC Member and PLAN Commander, spoke at a meeting on the PLAN's anti-piracy operations in the Gulf of Aden and referred to "close coordination" between the PLAN and shipping companies, and Ministries of Foreign Affairs and Transportation. In April 2011, the PLAN held a military-civilian exercise in the South China Sea. The next month, the Deputy Director of CMS forces referred to facing foreign "naval exercises" in 2010 in the Yellow Sea. The PLA's 2010 Defense White Paper of March 2011 asserted coordination and control between the PLA and other forces. In June 2011, the PLA held an exercise with CMS forces for the first time near Hainan Island. In March 2012, the PRC's National Administration of Surveying, Mapping, and Geoinformation (NASMG) announced a (continued...)

As the PLAN sails farther from China's coast on long-distance training or operations, the PLAN could pay more attention to freedom of navigation for its ships as well as foreign ships in a manner consistent with international law, instead of contradictory stances for PLAN ships and for foreign ships. The PLAN conducted military activities in the **EEZs** of other nations without their permission, including several operations in the U.S. EEZs of Hawaii and Guam in 2012 (including during the RIMPAC 2012 exercise).[67] On November 28 and December 10, 2012, the official *Xinhua* agency reported that PLAN ships sailed through straits near Japan's islands to and from training in the Western Pacific Ocean, arguing that other countries should respect the PLA's freedom of navigation and overflight in accordance with international law. In May 2013, the PLA's spokesman acknowledged that submarines may navigate freely in international waters.

PACOM Commander, Admiral Samuel Locklear, testified to the House Armed Services Committee on March 5, 2013, that there continued to be instances in which the PLA conducted unsafe or unprofessional maneuvers to impede U.S. forces operating legally in international air and maritime areas. On July 3, PRC media showed a video of a CMS ship that confronted the USS *Impeccable* on June 21 as operating outside its rights, even though it was about 100 miles from China's coast in the East China Sea. Later in July, Admiral Locklear said that U.S. and PLA forces have conducted operations around each other in an increasingly professional manner. Still, Locklear acknowledged continued disagreement about interpretations of activities in EEZs, while he argued against nations trying to control EEZs that cover one-third of oceans.[68]

(...continued)

working group to coordinate among 13 agencies in geographical surveys to map China's claims, first in the South China Sea and then also in the East China Sea (particularly concerning the Spratly and Senkaku Islands). On September 27, the Defense Ministry's spokesman said that the PLA ties its readiness to cooperating closely with CMS, FLEC, and other forces to provide support for the government's enforcement of laws at sea, fishing, oil and gas development, and other activities. Indeed, on October 19, ships and aircraft from the PLAN, FLEC, and CMS held an exercise, simulating actions against foreign ships. On January 19, 2013, a PLAN frigate directed a radar at a Japanese Maritime Self-Defense Force (MSDF) helicopter over the East China Sea. On January 30, another PLAN frigate directed its fire control radar at a Japanese MSDF destroyer. On February 4, Qi Jianguo, a PLA Deputy Chief of General Staff, convened a meeting held by the PLA's GSD and other unnamed government agencies on cooperation in maritime "struggles" and maritime security. On February 19, the State Oceanic Administration (SOA) and PLAN held a conference in Beijing (with PLAN Deputy Commander Ding Yiping attending). On March 10, the PRC announced that the maritime law enforcement forces (other than those under the Ministry of Transportation) would be reorganized as a new Coast Guard under the administration of the SOA and the direction of the MPS. A coordinating body, the State Maritime Committee, would be set up in the reorganization of CMS, PAP, FLEC, and Customs forces into the China Coast Guard. These developments appeared linked to the reported increased coordination since 2012 by top leader Xi Jinping, who reportedly has headed a Leading Small Group on Maritime Security. On April 23, over 40 PLAAF fighters, including Su-27 and Su-30 fighters, flew near the Senkaku Islands, while eight CMS ships entered Japan's claimed territorial waters around the islands, and Japan scrambled F-15 fighters. A later PRC CCTV report, apparently reporting on this drill, said that the PLAAF simulated precision strikes against land and maritime targets. Another CCTV report said that the PLAN's School for NCOs started training CMS personnel. On May 10, the Philippines protested to the PRC over the presence of two CMS ships and a PLAN ship near Second Thomas Shoal. Among other actions, in August 2013, the China Coast Guard started to "patrol" in claimed "territorial waters" around the North Luconia and South Luconia Reefs, close to Malaysia. On January 26, 2014, PLAN ships "patrolled" James Shoal (Zengmu) as the "southernmost part of China's territory," though it is a submerged reef 50 miles from Malaysia.

[67] Secretary of Defense, "Annual Report to Congress on Military and Security Developments Involving the PRC, 2013," May 2013. At the Shangri-la Dialogue in June, PLA Senior Colonel Zhou Bo said that the PLA Navy has sent ships to conduct reconnaissance in U.S. EEZs, according to *Defense News*, June 10, 2013.

[68] *Jane's Defense Weekly*, July 10, 2013; Defense Department, news briefing with Admiral Samuel Locklear III, July 11, 2013; *Washington Times*, July 17, 2013.

The U.S. military and the PLA could discuss the PRC's straight **baselines** drawn around islands, such as the baselines published for Hainan Island and Paracel Islands in the South China Sea in May 1996 and the Senkaku Islands in the East China Sea in September 2012. In March 2013, the United States protested to the PRC for its use of straight baselines around the Senkaku Islands as inconsistent with international law and impinging on the rights, freedoms, and uses of the sea under the Law of the Sea, while not taking a position on the ultimate sovereignty of the islands. Since the PRC is not an archipelagic country, it is not allowed to draw straight archipelagic baselines. The U.S. Navy may conduct operations to assert **freedom of navigation (FON)** to show that the United States does not recognize claims that are inconsistent with international law. In the annual report submitted to Congress two months later, the Defense Department criticized the PRC for using improperly drawn straight baselines around the Senkaku Islands and adding to the PRC's network of maritime claims that are inconsistent with international law.

In August 2013, Defense Secretary Chuck Hagel hosted PRC Defense Minister, General Chang Wanquan, and announced agreement with Xi Jinping's proposal to President Obama at their summit in June for new Working Groups on notifications of major military activities and standards of behavior for air and naval activities. An issue is whether to follow the PLA's mode of discussing bilateral rules or standards, rather than adherence to international rules worldwide.

Some progress might have resulted from the U.S. and other foreign pressure on the PLA to stress safety and prevention of collisions. In September 2012, even as a plenary meeting of the MMCA was held, the PLAN blocked adoption of a Code for Unalerted Encounters at Sea (CUES) at the Western Pacific Naval Symposium (**WPNS**) in Malaysia.[69] At the WPNS in China in April 2014, the PLAN and other navies finally approved **CUES** (changed to Code for Unplanned Encounters at Sea) to set procedures for safety (e.g., to avoid collisions) and communication at sea. The CUES stated that WPNS navies are expected to comply with the long-existing 1972 International Regulations for Preventing Collisions at Sea (**COLREGS**). PLAN Commander Admiral Wu Shengli spoke to commanders of foreign navies at WPNS and commended the new CUES for preventing incidents at sea and in the air but did not mention the COLREGS. CMC Vice Chairman, General Fan Changlong, met with WPNS attendees but did not cite the CUES.[70] An issue remains about whether the PLAN adheres to the COLREGS as well as CUES.

Defense Policy Coordination Talks (DPCT)

In early 2005, U.S. defense and PLA officials held a Special Policy Dialogue to discuss policy disputes and end an impasse in talks over safety and operational concerns under the MMCA. The separate discussions continued in the first Defense Policy Coordination Talks (DPCT) held in Washington in December 2006. The first combined exercise held under the MMCA, a search and rescue exercise (SAREX), did not take place until the fall of 2006, after eight years of talks. By 2007, the MMCA's status and value were in greater doubt, and no MMCA working groups or plenary meetings took place that year.

On February 25-26, 2008, in Qingdao, PACOM's Director for Strategic Planning and Policy (J-5), USMC Major General Thomas Conant, and PLA Navy Deputy Chief of Staff Zhang Leiyu led an annual meeting under the MMCA, the first since 2006. The PLA sought to amend the MMCA.

---

[69] *Jane's Defense Weekly*, September 28, 2012.

[70] WPNS, CUES, April 22, 2014, Qingdao, China; *Jiefangjun Bao [Liberation Army Daily]*, April 23 and 24, 2014.

The U.S. side opposed PLA proposals to discuss policy differences at the MMCA meetings and to plan details of future military exercises.[71] The PLA and U.S. military have clashed over the PRC's disputes with foreign countries over the freedom of navigation in the high seas.

By 2011, the PLA seemed to downgrade the DPCT as merely "working-level" talks between the U.S. Deputy Assistant Secretary of Defense and the Director of the PLA's Foreign Affairs Office. The practice was at odds with the reaffirmation during Secretary Gates' visit in early 2011, when Defense Minister Liang Guanglie agreed that the DCT, DPCT, and MMCA were important talks.

Incidents at Sea (INCSEA) Protocol

For his nomination hearing to be the PACOM Commander on March 8, 2007, Admiral Timothy Keating answered questions from the Senate Armed Services Committee by claiming that a dangerous incident similar to the EP-3 crisis would be "less likely." He also proposed negotiating with the PLA an "Incidents at Sea" (INCSEA) protocol, like the 1972 one with the Soviet Union.

After the Pentagon reported in March 2009 that PRC ships were aggressively harassing U.S. ocean surveillance ships (including the USNS Impeccable) in the Yellow Sea and South China Sea, some observers raised again the issue of whether to agree with the PLA on an INCSEA. For example, retired Rear Admiral Eric McVaden suggested that an INCSEA could compel China's top leaders to agree to avoid collisions or escalations of tensions, as well as provide rules and a safety valve. However, skeptics said that the question was not whether there was an agreement or dialogue. For example, former Deputy Assistant Secretary of State Randy Schriver pointed out that the MMCA would have been called an INCSEA (but the United States wanted to avoid "Cold War connotations") and that the MMCA had limited usefulness because China has more interest in stopping U.S. reconnaissance than any interest in the agreement that it had signed. Thus, he contended that the MMCA already has provided the mechanism for dealing with incidents at sea. The problem has been that the PLA is not interested in a "rules-based, operator-to-operator approach to safety on the high seas."[72] In early 2011, Chief of Naval Operations (CNO) Gary Roughead explained another opposition to an INCSEA. Admiral Roughead said that an INCSEA with only the PLAN would result in a separate and exclusive agreement, set the PLA apart when all militaries ought to adhere to the same international "rules of the road," and define the relationship with the PLA as abnormal, aggressive, and a specter of that with the Soviet Union.[73]

Hotline, or Defense Telephone Link (DTL)

After staff-level preliminary discussions in 2003, Under Secretary of Defense Douglas Feith formally proposed a hotline for crisis management and confidence building with the PLA at the DCT in February 2004. However, the PLA did not give a positive signal until a defense ministerial conference in Singapore in June 2007, when Lieutenant General (LTG) Zhang Qinsheng, Deputy Chief of General Staff, said that the PLA would discuss such a hotline. During

---

[71] Major General Thomas Conant and Rear Admiral Zhang Leiyu, "Summary of Proceedings of the Annual Meeting Under the Agreement Between the Ministry of National Defense of the People's Republic of China and the Department of Defense of the United States of America on Establishing a Consultative Mechanism to Strengthen Military Maritime Safety," Qingdao, February 26, 2008.

[72] Quoted in the "Nelson Report," March 11, 2009.

[73] Quoted in an interview with the *Financial Times*, January 18, 2011.

Defense Secretary Gates' visit to China in November 2007, the PLA agreed in principle to set up a defense telephone link (DTL) with the Pentagon. The two sides signed an agreement in February 2008. In May 2008, PACOM's Commander, Admiral Keating, used the hotline in its first operational use to communicate with PLA Deputy Chief of General Staff Ma Xiaotian about the U.S. Air Force's use of two C-17 transports to deliver earthquake relief supplies to Sichuan.

However, during the confrontation in March 2009 when PRC ships aggressively harassed the U.S. surveillance ships, Secretary Gates told reporters on March 18, 2009, that he did not use the hotline. Indeed, not until May 2011 did the PLA agree to actually use the DTL, as promised by visiting Chief of General Staff Chen Bingde, according to Chairman of the Joint Chiefs of Staff Mullen's remarks on July 10, 2011. Further, some observers urged PACOM and the Pentagon to prepare transcripts of all uses of the DTL as records of communication with the PLA. Issues include whether to use the DTL for regular communication (e.g., about visits), transparency, and consultations with Congress and U.S. allies about these discussions. The Obama Administration shifted to use the "hotline" for routine discussions, not only in times of crises. In March 2013, General Dempsey, Chairman of the Joint Chiefs of Staff, talked on the phone with General Fang Fenghui, Chief of General Staff. The next month, Defense Secretary Chuck Hagel spoke on the phone to General Chang Wanquan, PRC Defense Minister. In May, General Dempsey again talked on the phone with General Fang. Defense officials have used the DTL at other times. In May 2014, Chairman of the Joint Chiefs of Staff Martin Dempsey discussed with visiting Chief of General Staff Fang Fenghui a U.S. proposal to upgrade the DTL to video teleconference.

Air Traffic Control (ATC)

Another area for possible improved communication and prevention of accidents is air traffic control in China, which is controlled by the PLA Air Force. In December 2006, the PLA suddenly shut down the busy Pudong International Airport near Shanghai and at least three other airports under the Nanjing Military Region, ostensibly for training.[74] In December 2010, PRC media revealed the establishment of a new national air traffic control system and that it was one of the high-priority, militarily-significant, and centrally-directed "863 Projects."

Sanya Initiative and Other Informal Talks

Some believe that more dialogue, even unofficial talks involving U.S. retired senior generals and admirals or nongovernmental "track two" researchers, could be useful to build understanding and avoid conflict with the PLA.[75] Others question the use of private channels that could undermine or influence U.S. policies, send mixed messages, and confuse unofficial with official work, particularly since the PLA would have only ostensibly unofficial representatives. In January 2010, a delegation from the China Foundation for International and Strategic Studies (CFISS) visited Washington with a delegation that included PLA major generals and other officers. They got meetings with Under Secretaries of Defense, the Principal Deputy Assistant Secretary of Defense for Asian and Pacific Security Affairs, Deputy Secretary of State, Assistant Secretary of State for East Asian and Pacific Affairs, and National Security Council officials.[76]

---

[74] Bruce Stanley, "China's Congested Skies," *Wall Street Journal*, February 16, 2007.

[75] Michael Swaine (Carnegie Endowment), "Avoiding U.S.-China Military Rivalry," *Diplomat*, February 16, 2011.

[76] The National Committee on U.S.-China Relations hosted the Track II Dialogue on Northeast Asian Security.

Even for dealing with possible crises, Admiral Keating revealed in 2007 that he used an unofficial network of retired Admirals who had commanded PACOM and met with PLA commanders.[77] The PLA has pursued this track, including a visit to Beijing in November 2010 of a group led by retired PACOM Commander and Admiral Thomas Fargo. Their host, General Li Jinai, a CMC Member and Director of the GPD, asked the visitors to use their "personal influence" on mil-to-mil ties. The China Association for International Friendly Contact (CAIFC) sponsored the group.

In addition, a "Sanya Initiative" (named for the first such informal dialogue at the Sanya resort on Hainan Island) began in February 2008. Xiong Guangkai (President of the China Institute for International Strategic Studies and former Deputy Chief of General Staff in charge of intelligence) led the PLA side. Bill Owens (retired admiral and former Vice Chairman of the Joint Chiefs of Staff) led the U.S. side. The PLA side asked the U.S. participants to help with PRC objections to U.S. policies and laws: namely the Taiwan Relations Act (TRA), Pentagon's report to Congress on PRC Military Power, and legal restrictions on military contacts in the NDAA for FY2000.[78] A second meeting was held on October 16-22, 2009, at PACOM in Honolulu, Washington, and New York. Despite the unofficial talks, PACOM Commander (Admiral Tim Keating), Chairman of the Joint Chiefs of Staff (Admiral Mike Mullen), Vice Chairman of the Joint Chief of Staff (General James Cartwright), Deputy Secretary of Defense William Lynn, Secretary of State Hillary Clinton, and Assistant Secretary of State Kurt Campbell met with the Sanya group. Afterwards, Bill Owens published an opinion to oppose the TRA as harming the relationship with China that has rising wealth and influence.[79] Observers noted Owen's business interests in China as a Managing Director of AEA Investors in Hong Kong. In May 2010, Owens told the press that he was "grieved" by mil-to-mil suspensions over arms sales to Taiwan, including postponement of another meeting of his Sanya Initiative, when he met with CMC Vice Chairman Xu Caihou in Beijing.[80] Owens and his group went to Beijing for a third round of the Sanya talks in October 2010, and they met with CMC Member and GPD Director Li Jinai. In June 2012, Owens led six retired generals and admirals to meet with retired PLA generals (without Xiong Guangkai) in Annapolis and Washington. They met with Senators Carl Levin and John McCain of the Senate Armed Services Committee; Representatives Charles Boustany and Rick Larsen of the U.S.-China Working Group; Assistant Secretary of Defense Mark Lippert and Lieutenant General (LTG) Terry Wolff; and Assistant Secretary of State Campbell.[81]

On December 20, 2012, Bill Owens and three retired Generals (Kevin Chilton, Michael Moseley, and Peter Pace) visited Beijing for another round. They met with CMC Vice Chairman Xu Qiliang, and CMC Member and GPD Director Zhang Yang. Owens again visited Beijing in June and December 2013, meeting with GPD Director Zhang Yang.

---

[77] Forum on "Evolving and Enhancing Military Relations," George Bush U.S.-China Relations Conference 2007, Washington, DC, October 24, 2007.

[78] *People's Daily*, February 24, 2008; Sanya Initiative, "Key Outcomes and Summary Report," March 2008; Jennifer Harper, "Retired U.S. Brass to Defend Chinese Military," *Washington Times*, April 4, 2008; CSIS, "A Briefing on the Sanya Initiative," June 6, 2008; author's consultations, March 2009.

[79] Bill Owens, "America Must Start Treating China as a Friend," *Financial Times*, November 17, 2009.

[80] *South China Morning Post*, May 23, 2010; *Xinhua*, May 26, 2010.

[81] "Fostering U.S.-China Military-to-Military Relations," East West Institute (EWI), New York, June 28, 2012.

Civilian Control over PLA and Civil-Military Coordination

Related to the U.S. security interest in preventing inadvertent or predictable conflict or crises with China, the Obama Administration has sought "comprehensive" engagement and bilateral dialogues that advance coordination between the PLA and the PRC's top leadership or its civilian officials in foreign affairs, including through the structure of the S&ED (as discussed above on "Options"). Another goal has been the expansion of cooperation in overlapping interests.

As mentioned above, when the PLA declined to host Defense Secretary Gates in 2010, he implied a divide between the PLA and the top PRC leadership. Then, on July 20, 2010, the United States and Republic of Korea (ROK) announced combined military exercises in the seas to the west and east of the ROK, commonly called the Yellow Sea and Sea of Japan, in response to North Korea's attack on the South Korean naval ship *Cheonan* on March 26 that killed 46 sailors. However, even before the announcement and even though the exercises were not about China, PLA General Ma Xiaotian on July 1 expressed "opposition" to the expected U.S.-ROK exercises in the Yellow Sea. A week after that, the Foreign Ministry shifted from "concern" to "opposition" to any foreign military ships and aircraft entering or flying over the Yellow Sea. The PRC especially objected to the aircraft carrier USS *George Washington* joining exercises in the Yellow Sea, even off the coast of South Korea. Still, while more assertive in its voice on policy, the PLA's resistance or opposition might not be a constant or dominant voice in PRC policymaking, as seen in the belated invitation to Gates for his visit in January 2011. After North Korea again attacked South Korea on November 23, 2010, launching artillery on Yeonpyeoung Island that killed two South Korean marines and even two civilians, the PLA was relatively quiet in public after the U.S. and ROK announcement the next day that the USS *George Washington* would exercise with the ROK navy in the Yellow Sea from November 28 to December 1, as first indicated back in July. Meanwhile, the PRC Foreign Ministry shifted its stance from "taking note" of the U.S.-ROK exercise to "opposing" any military action in "China's" EEZ without China's permission. Secretary Gates pointedly asked Hu Jintao about a test of a J-20 stealth fighter conducted during Gates' visit in January 2011, and Gates said that Hu seemed surprised when asked about the test. Gates clarified on June 2 that he did not believe that the PLA was not responsive to PRC leaders. He said that the PLA did not seem to go out of its way to inform regularly the political leadership.

In the two U.S.-PRC Joint Statements of November 2009 and January 2011, top PRC leader Hu Jintao agreed to state with President Obama that "China welcomes the United States as an Asia-Pacific nation that contributes to peace, stability, and prosperity in the region." In contrast, the PLA in March 2011 issued the 2010 Defense White Paper that did not include that sentiment but did print implied and explicit criticism of the United States. The Joint Statement of January 2011 did not note a "strategic dialogue" that Gates proposed earlier that month during his visit.

However, questions were not new about the PLA's actions separate from top PRC policymaking. A more crucial concern about Hu Jintao's command of the PLA already was raised after the summit in April 2006 at which he discussed with President Bush about starting a strategic nuclear dialogue, but the Commander of the PLA Second Artillery has declined to visit. Then, in January 2007, the PLA conducted its first successful, direct-ascent anti-satellite (ASAT) weapon test, but the Foreign Ministry remained silent to the world about it for 12 days.[82] There could have been a division of labor where PLA and CPC leaderships pursued parallel relationships with foreign countries, not only with the United States. For example, in May 2003, PLA General Cao

---

[82] See CRS Report RS22652, *China's Anti-Satellite Weapon Test*, by Shirley A. Kan.

Gangchuan (a CMC Vice Chairman and Defense Minister) and PRC President Hu Jintao simultaneously visited Moscow, Russia, but PRC media reported their visits separately with no joint meetings. There could have been a lack of *coordination* between the PLA and civilian officials in the weaker Foreign Ministry, though the CMC Chairman and CPC General-Secretary remained in ultimate *control* of the PLA. Moreover, the PRC's priority programs for military modernization, including ASAT weapons, have existed for many years and have been coordinated and controlled by a top-level military-civilian Central Special Committee (CSC) in line with the PRC's long-standing stress on "Military-Civilian Integration."[83] Another assessment focused on the lack of military-civilian coordination at the lower levels, especially on foreign policy.[84] In any case, by 2010, U.S. officials noted the PLA's stronger voice and capabilities, raising concern about the PLA's influence on China's adherence to established international laws and norms.

The PLA can coordinate with civilian authorities when it chooses to do so. In March 2009, PRC Y-12 maritime surveillance aircraft, a PLAN frigate, PRC patrol and intelligence collection ships, and trawlers coordinated in increasingly aggressive and dangerous harassment of unarmed U.S. ocean surveillance ships, the USNS *Victorious* and USNS *Impeccable*, during routine operations in international waters in the Yellow Sea and South China Sea. In January 2011, Wu Shengli, CMC Member and PLAN Commander, spoke at a meeting on the PLAN's "escort" mission (vs. U.S. counter-piracy operations) in the Gulf of Aden and referred to "close coordination" between the PLAN and shipping companies, and Ministries of Foreign Affairs and Transportation. In another example, in April 2011, the PLAN held a military-civilian exercise in the South China Sea. The next month, the Deputy Director of the civilian China Marine Surveillance (CMS) forces referred to facing foreign "naval exercises" in 2010 in the Yellow Sea.[85] The Defense White Paper of March 2011 noted coordination and control between the PLA and other agencies.

Secretary of State Clinton gave a speech on April 10, 2012, stressing that "China is not the Soviet Union," "we are not on the brink of a new Cold War in Asia," and "this is not 1912 when friction between a declining Britain and a rising Germany set the stage for global conflict." Apparently responding positively at the S&ED on May 3 in Beijing, PRC leader Hu Jintao called for a "new type of great power relationship" that is reassuring to both countries and to others. General Liang Guanglie, as the Defense Minister, visited the United States on May 4-10, where he echoed Hu by saying that "China and the United States should build a new type of state-to-state relationship that is not in the stereotype that the two major powers are predestined to engage into confrontation or conflict." The PLA supports a positive tone for U.S.-PRC ties, in line with top CPC leaders.

Unlike Hu's visit to Moscow 10 years before, Xi Jinping visited in March 2013 and Defense Minister Chang Wanquan joined him, at least in a military meeting. However, that change could have been because Xi paid the first visit by a PRC head of state to the Russian Defense Ministry.

---

[83] Tai Ming Cheung, *Fortifying China* (Cornell University Press, 2009); Trefor Moss, "Rumours of PLA Dissent Are Greatly Exaggerated," *Jane's Defence Weekly*, February 23, 2011. A PRC researcher close to the PLA conceded the need for improved coordination in foreign policy to manage crises, Zhang Tuosheng, in *Shijie Zhishi* in January 2011.

[84] Michael Swaine, "China's Assertive Behavior; Part Three: The Role of the Military in Foreign Policy," *China Leadership Monitor*, Winter 2011.

[85] *Jiefangjun Bao*, January 15, 2011; "Military Report," *CCTV-7*, April 23, 2011; *China Daily*, May 2, 2011.

Transparency, Reciprocity, and Information-Exchange

Critics of military exchanges with China have charged that the United States gained limited information about the PLA, while granting greater access to the PLA than the access we received. A related question in the debate has concerned the extent to which the issues of reciprocity and transparency should affect or impede efforts to increase mutual understanding with the PLA.

According to the Pentagon's report to Congress of January 2001, in 1998, the PLA denied requests by the Chief of Staff of the Air Force (CSAF) to fly in an SU-27 fighter, see integration of the SU-27s into units, and learn about development of the F-10 fighter. Also in 1998, the PLA denied the Defense Secretary's request to visit China's National Command Center. Still, the PLA requested access to U.S. exercises showing warfighting capabilities, with two cases of U.S. denial in 1999: PLA requests to send observers to the U.S. Army's National Training Center (NTC) at Fort Irwin, CA, and to the Red Flag air combat training exercise at Nellis Air Force Base, NV.

Regarding controversial access to the U.S. Army's NTC, visits by the PLA in the 1990s included those in November 1994 and December 1997.[86] Then, in December 1998, the Army reportedly resisted a PLA request for greater, unprecedented access to the NTC in 1999, because the PLA asked for access greater than that granted to other countries, the PLA would gain information to enhance its warfighting, and the PLA was unlikely to reciprocate with similar access for the U.S. military. The PLA wanted to observe, with direct access, the 3rd Infantry Division (Mechanized) and the 82nd Airborne Division in a training exercise. Army officials reportedly felt pressured by Admiral Prueher at PACOM and Secretary Cohen to grant the request. In the end, the Pentagon announced on March 17, 1999, that it denied the PLA's request.[87]

The Defense Department's 2003 report to Congress on PRC military power charged that "since the 1980s, U.S. military exchange delegations to China have been shown only 'showcase' units, never any advanced units or any operational training or realistic exercises."[88] However, a Rand study in 2004 argued that the DOD's statement "appears to be inaccurate." Rand reported that between 1993 and 1999, U.S. visitors went to 51 PLA units. (PLA delegations visited 71 U.S. military units between 1994 and 1999.) The report recommended that "the best way of dealing with the reciprocity and transparency issue is to remove it as an issue." It called for proper planning and a focus on educational exchanges.[89] Still, reciprocal exchanges at military educational institutions has been challenged by the PLA's separation of foreign military and PLA students, with foreign students grouped in their own classes and facilities, while U.S. schools tended to integrate U.S. and foreign students. It was not until March 2009, that the PLA reportedly started to follow international practice to mix foreign and PLA students in the same class, at the Air Force Command College of the PLAAF.[90]

---

[86] The PLA's visit to the NTC in November 1994 was not the first time that the PLA observed U.S. military training at Fort Irwin. In August 1985, the United States allowed the PLA to observe military training at Fort Benning, GA; Fort Bragg, NC; and Fort Irwin, CA. See Colonel Jer Donald Get, "What's With the Relationship Between America's Army and China's PLA?" Army War College monograph, September 15, 1996.

[87] Sean Naylor, "Chinese Denied Full Access to the NTC," *Army Times*, March 29, 1999.

[88] Department of Defense, "Report on PRC Military Power," July 2003.

[89] Kevin Pollpeter, "U.S. China Security Management: Assessing the Military-to-Military Relationship," RAND Corporation, 2004.

[90] *Jiefangjun Bao [Liberation Army Daily]*, July 16, 2010.

In 2005, the PRC did not allow U.S. forces to observe the major combined PLA-Russian military exercise, "Peace Mission 2005," and prohibited U.S. participation in the multilateral humanitarian exercise in Hong Kong, in which U.S. forces had joined for years in the past.[91] Still, PACOM Commander, Admiral Fallon, invited PLA observers to the U.S. "Valiant Shield" exercise that brought three aircraft carriers to waters off Guam in June 2006. In August 2007, U.S. observers were not invited to monitor the PRC-Russian combined exercise "Peace Mission 2007."

Nonetheless, U.S. participants in contacts with the PLA have reported gaining insights into PLA capabilities and concepts. The record of military contacts since 1993 (in the **Appendix** of this report) showed some instances when the PLA allowed U.S. officials to be first-time foreign visitors with first-time "**unprecedented access**." These examples included the following:

- Satellite Control Center in Xian (1995)

- Guangzhou Military Region headquarters (1997)

- Beijing Military Region's Air Defense Command Center (1998)

- 47th Group Army (1998)

- Armored Force Engineering Academy (2000)

- Training base in Inner Mongolia (2003), with multinational access

- Zhanjiang, homeport of the PLAN's South Sea Fleet (2003)

- Beijing Aerospace Control Center (2004)

- 2nd Artillery (missile corps) headquarters (2005)

- 39th Group Army (2006)

- FB-7 fighter at 28th Air Division (2006)

- Su-27 fighter and T-99 tank (2007)

- Jining Air Force Base (2007)

- Song-class submarine and Luzhou-class destroyer (2007)

- CSS-7 (M-11) short-range ballistic missile and Yuan-class submarine (2011)

- GZMR's 121st Infantry Division of the 41st Group Army (2012)

- Aircraft carrier (*Liaoning*) at Qingdao (2014).

Tension Reduction over Taiwan

Tensions over Taiwan have continued to flare since the mid-1990s, with many observers fearing the possibility of war looming between the United States and China—two nuclear powers. In April 2004, Assistant Secretary of State James Kelly testified to Congress that U.S. efforts at deterring China's coercion "might fail" if Beijing becomes convinced that it must stop Taiwan from advancing on a course toward permanent separation from China.[92] Kelly also noted that the

---

[91] Assistant Secretary of Defense Peter Rodman, remarks to the U.S.-China Economic and Security Review Commission, March 16, 2006.

[92] Testimony at a hearing on "The Taiwan Relations Act: The Next 25 Years," before the House International Relations (continued...)

PRC leadership accelerated the PLA buildup after 1999. The Pentagon reported to Congress in May 2004 that the PLA has "accelerated" modernization, including a missile buildup, in response to concerns about Taiwan.[93]

Under the Taiwan Relations Act (TRA), P.L. 96-8, that has governed U.S. policy toward Taiwan since 1979, Congress has oversight of the President's management of the cross-strait situation under the rubric of the "one China" policy.[94] While considering contacts with the PLA, the United States, after the 1995-1996 Taiwan Strait Crisis, has increased arms sales to and ties with Taiwan's military.[95] Policy considerations include offering arms sales and cooperation to help Taiwan's self-defense; securing leverage over Beijing and Taipei; deterring aggression or coercion; discouraging provocations from Beijing or Taipei; and supporting cross-strait dialogue and confidence-building measures (CBMs). In educational exchanges with the PLA, questions have concerned whether to allow PLA officers to attend U.S. military academies, colleges, or universities, and how that change could affect attendees from Taiwan's military; and whether to allow attendees from Taiwan at PACOM's Asia-Pacific Center for Security Studies (APCSS).

Concerning the APCSS courses in Honolulu, the Bush Administration's policy change to allow attendance from Taiwan affected the PLA's attendance and interactions among the U.S., PRC, and other Asian militaries. In November 2001, the Department of Defense directed APCSS to allow people from Taiwan to participate in courses and conferences. Acknowledging the potential difficulty for continuing participation by the PLA, the policy called for alternating invitations to the PRC and Taiwan. In the summer of 2002, three fellows from Taiwan attended the Executive Course, the first time that Taiwan sent students to APCSS. Ostensibly objecting to alternating attendance with Taiwan's representatives, the PLA stopped sending representatives to APCSS, after attending courses from 1999 to mid-2002. Nonetheless, by 2010, the U.S. military assessed that Taiwan's attendance was a convenient excuse and complaint, even as the PRC has sent non-PLA students to APCSS since 2008 (and APCSS has complied with the PRC's goals and control of attendance by a PRC organization). Moreover, the PLA's NDU had set up its own International Symposium Course (ISC) in 1999 modeled after APCSS to "train" foreign military officers such that the PLA controls discussions between its officers and foreign counterparts.[96]

While the Mutual Defense Treaty of 1954 terminated at the end of 1979 and the TRA does not commit the United States to defend Taiwan, the TRA states that it is U.S. policy, *inter alia*:

- to consider any non-peaceful efforts to determine the future of Taiwan, including boycotts or embargoes, a threat to the peace and security of the Western Pacific region and of "grave concern" to the United States;

- to provide Taiwan with arms of a defensive character (making available to Taiwan such defense articles and defense services in such quantity as may be necessary to enable Taiwan to maintain a sufficient self-defense capability);

(...continued)

Committee, April 21, 2004.

[93] Defense Department, "Annual Report on PRC Military Power," May 29, 2004.

[94] See CRS Report RL30341, *China/Taiwan: Evolution of the "One China" Policy—Key Statements from Washington, Beijing, and Taipei*, by Shirley A. Kan.

[95] See CRS Report RL30957, *Taiwan: Major U.S. Arms Sales Since 1990*, by Shirley A. Kan.

[96] Consultation at the Biennial Conference at APCSS on July 16-18, 2002, and with former PACOM staff; Colonel (retired) Frank Miller's presentation at Army War College, October 2010; consultation at PACOM, November 2010.

- to maintain the U.S. capacity to resist any resort to force or other forms of coercion that would jeopardize the security, or the social or economic system, of the people on Taiwan.

There is a question about the extent of the U.S. role in supporting cross-strait dialogue. In Shanghai in July 2000, visiting Secretary of Defense Cohen said that the Clinton Administration viewed the newly elected President Chen Shui-bian of Taiwan as offering hope for cross-strait reconciliation. Cohen stepped out of the narrow mil-to-mil context and met with Wang Daohan, chairman of the PRC's Association for Relations Across the Taiwan Strait (ARATS). This meeting raised questions about the U.S. role in more actively encouraging cross-strait talks. Cohen said that Chen showed flexibility after becoming president and that there was a window of opportunity for changes.[97] In contrast, in Beijing in February 2004, visiting Under Secretary of Defense Feith said he did not discuss the contentious issue raised by PLA leaders "at length" concerning referendums in Taiwan—an issue over which the PRC threatened to use force. Feith said he did not discuss the issue because it was not defense-related.[98]

There are complications in consideration of the question of Taiwan in the U.S.-PRC military relationship. Not discussing Taiwan leaves the primary dispute subject to misperception or miscalculation. However, linking the Taiwan question can raise tensions and frustrations over a disagreement that military exchanges cannot solve. A 2007 study co-authored by former PACOM Commander Dennis Blair called for discussion of the PLA's missile buildup against Taiwan and greater efforts to reduce tensions across the Taiwan Strait.[99]

The PLA has suspended military exchanges in retaliation for steps in U.S. policy toward Taiwan, especially continued arms sales. However, even as the PLA signaled its displeasure and urged U.S. cooperation in "peace and stability" in the Taiwan Strait, cutting off exchanges played a counterproductive role by raising U.S.-PRC tension. Moreover, the PRC's implicit linkage has targeted the U.S. Navy in particular, precisely the service advocating engagement with the PLA.

After Taiwan's President Chen Shui-bian proposed in June 2007 that Taiwan hold a referendum on membership in the U.N. under the name "Taiwan" on the day of the next presidential election (scheduled for March 22, 2008), Beijing opposed it as a step toward Taiwan's de jure independence. While joining the PRC in opposing the referendum, the Bush Administration continued the U.S. policy of providing some security assistance to Taiwan. After notifications to Congress of arms sales to Taiwan in September and November 2007, the PRC protested by refusing to hold military-to-military exchanges, including an annual MMCA meeting scheduled for October 2007. The PRC also denied port visits at Hong Kong in November 2007 by U.S. Navy minesweepers in distress (USS *Patriot* and USS *Guardian*) and by the carrier group led by the USS *Kitty Hawk* for the Thanksgiving holiday and family reunions, leading to official protests by the Pentagon to the PLA.

After sailing away from the denied port call in Hong Kong toward Japan, the USS *Kitty Hawk* sailed through the Taiwan Strait, raising objections in China with claims in PRC media of the

---

[97] Department of Defense, "Secretary Cohen's Press Conference at the Shanghai Stock Exchange," Shanghai, China, July 14, 2000.

[98] Joe McDonald (AP), "Feith Voices Concern Over Chinese Missiles," *Army Times*, February 11, 2004.

[99] Dennis Blair and Carla Hills, co-chairs of a task force at the Council on Foreign Relations, "U.S.-China Relations: An Affirmative Agenda, A Responsible Course," April 10, 2007.

strait as China's "internal waterway." When asked at a news conference in Beijing on January 15, 2008, visiting PACOM Commander, Admiral Keating said, "we don't need China's permission to go through the Taiwan Strait. It's international water. We will exercise our free right of passage whenever and wherever we choose as we have done repeatedly in the past and we'll do in the future." Two days later, when asked whether ships need the PRC's permission to sail through the Taiwan Strait, China's foreign ministry spokesperson did not reject the idea of permission from Beijing while claiming the strait as a "highly sensitive area."

After the Bush Administration notified Congress of some pending arms sales to Taiwan on October 3, 2008, the PLA suspended some but not all military exchanges and nonproliferation talks. The Defense Department spokesman said that the PRC canceled or postponed several meetings in "continued politicization" of the military-to-military exchanges.[100]

After tentative support in 2008 in both Beijing and Taipei for cross-strait confidence building measures (CBMs), PACOM's Admiral Keating raised the question of a U.S. role when he offered in February 2009 to host talks between the PLA and Taiwan's military.[101] However, Reagan's "Six Assurances" to Taiwan in 1982 included one of not "mediating" between Beijing and Taipei.

Meanwhile, President Obama did not notify Congress of any major Foreign Military Sales (FMS) to Taiwan in 2009. After President Obama's five notifications on January 29, 2010, the PRC threatened the next day to respond in four ways: postpone "partial" military-to-military exchanges; postpone deputy ministerial level meetings on international security, arms control, and weapons nonproliferation; impose sanctions on U.S. defense firms involved in the arms sales to Taiwan; and react in interactions on international and regional problems. The State Department issued a statement, regretting that the PRC government announced plans to curtail military-to-military and other security-related exchanges and to take action against U.S. firms that supply defensive articles to Taiwan, because U.S. policy contributes to stability and security.[102] The PRC's immediate response was the postponement of Deputy Secretary of State James Steinberg's meetings in Beijing in February (that later took place in early March). The threat to U.S. firms was new in public but already existed and remained vague (with possible, partial impact on two companies, Boeing and General Electric) and risked backfiring on Beijing (in trade or other ties). Further, the PRC Embassy in Washington even called at least one U.S. defense firm's executive directly on a personal phone on a weekend in early February with an implied warning. The company countered that the PRC already had a "blacklist" against some U.S. firms, the embassy's contact was highly inappropriate, and the senior diplomat should direct the PRC's messages instead to the State Department. The firm informed State of the harassment of U.S. executives.

The impact on mil-to-mil meetings was mixed, since there were tentative major mutual visits in discussion but they were not scheduled and then canceled by the PLA. As the Chairman of the Joint Chiefs of Staff Admiral Mike Mullen said at a press conference on February 22, he was not aware of any mil-to-mil activities that had been ongoing and then called off. The PRC allowed a port visit (by the USS *Nimitz*) in Hong Kong in February. In the spring, there were minor meetings at which the PLA declined to participate (such as a conference at the Naval War College) or host (such as visits by the students of the National War College and CAPSTONE class for flag/general officers). Yet, Deputy Assistant Secretary of Defense for POW/MIA

---

[100] Statement quoted in "China Cancels Military Contacts with U.S. in Protest," *AP*, October 6, 2008.

[101] Quoted in "Optimism Grows for U.S.-China Military Talks," *New York Times*, February 19, 2009.

[102] Quoted by *Reuters*, January 30, 2010.

Personnel Affairs Bob Newberry visited Beijing in April to discuss with PLA officials accounting for missing personnel. In May, PACOM Commander Admiral Robert Willard and Assistant Secretary of Defense Wallace Gregson visited Beijing for the Strategic and Economic Dialogue and met with PLA Deputy Chief of General Staff Ma Xiaotian (Air Force General) and Rear Admiral Guan Youfei who blasted the U.S. side for numerous faults.[103] In June, when Secretary Gates traveled to Singapore for the "Shangri-la Dialogue" of defense ministers, the PLA sent a lower-level official (Ma) to the meeting and declined to host Gates for a visit. Still, while the PLA and others pointed to U.S. arms sales as the reason for the PLA's snub, another factor could have been the timing of a visit, right after South Korea announced on May 20 the finding that North Korea sank the South Korean naval ship Cheonan on March 26. The PRC continued to support North Korea and could have found it useful also to blame U.S. arms sales to Taiwan. Defense Minister Liang Guanglie later attributed timing difficulties in not hosting Gates in June.[104] Also in June, a PLA attaché with the rank of Senior Colonel based in Washington spoke officially and in uniform at the U.S. Army Training and Doctrine Command (TRADOC) in Virginia. Finally, if the PLA believed that U.S. arms sales to Taiwan actually countered PRC interests, the PLA or the broader PRC authorities have not retaliated against Taiwan for requesting or buying defense items. PRC threats or steps have been directed against the United States but not Taiwan.

Meanwhile, the Obama Administration resurrected an approach from the Clinton Administration, as discussed above, whereby the mil-to-mil relationship involved PRC/CPC officials on Taiwan. In September 2010, Deputy Assistant Secretary of Defense Michael Schiffer visited Beijing to discuss military exchanges but also included a meeting at the Taiwan Affairs Office (TAO). At the same time, the PLA expressed the desire to resume all military-to-military exchanges.

After President Obama notified Congress of major arms sales to Taiwan on September 21, 2011, the PLA postponed the visits of the PACOM Commander (Admiral Robert Willard) and U.S. Army Band (to reciprocate for the PLA band's visit); a combined anti-piracy naval drill in the Gulf of Aden; and a combined medical rescue exercise with the PLA's naval hospital ship. That PLAN ship, named "Peace Ark," conducted an emergency medical drill in the Pacific Ocean on September 22, as it sailed to visit Latin American countries. Nonetheless, by December 2011, the PLA hosted in Beijing the 12th round of the Defense Consultative Talks (DCT).

Weapons Nonproliferation[105]

Despite long-term engagement with the PLA to seek cooperation in weapons nonproliferation, the United States continues to have concerns about and has imposed sanctions on PRC entities. China has close relationships with Pakistan, Iran, and the DPRK. China did not join in the U.S.-led Proliferation Security Initiative (PSI) announced in May 2003 (to interdict dangerous shipments).

There are concerns that China expanded nuclear cooperation with Pakistan, supported the DPRK, and could undermine sanctions against Iran (including in the oil/gas energy sector). In 2002-2008, the U.S. approach relied on China's influence on North Korea to dismantle its nuclear weapons. Beijing hosted the "Six-Party Talks" (last held in December 2008) with limited results. Since 2006, China's balanced approach has evolved to vote for some U.N. Security Council (UNSC)

---

[103] John Pomfret, "In Chinese Admiral's Outburst, a Lingering Distrust of U.S.," *Washington Post*, June 8, 2010.

[104] *Nihon Keizai Shimbun*, Tokyo, June 12, 2010.

[105] For further discussion, see CRS Report RL31555, *China and Proliferation of Weapons of Mass Destruction and Missiles: Policy Issues*, by Shirley A. Kan.

sanctions against missile or nuclear proliferation in North Korea and Iran. Some called for engaging more with Beijing to use its leverage against Pyongyang and Tehran. However, North Korea's nuclear tests in 2006, 2009, and 2013 have prompted greater debate about how to change China's calculus and the value of its role. Moreover, on December 11, 2012, North Korea conducted its first apparently successful test of the three-stage Taepo Dong-2 long-range missile, whose first stage fell into the Yellow Sea and second stage fell into the Philippine Sea and which launched an object into orbit. China agreed to sanctions in a balanced, incremental way, and questions remain about its implementation of agreed sanctions. China's approach has not shown fundamental changes toward Iran and North Korea. In a phone call in April 2013 with Defense Minister Chang Wanquan, Defense Secretary Chuck Hagel sought cooperation on North Korea's "growing threat" to the United States and our allies. In August, a member of the visiting PRC Defense Minister's delegation and the PLA's Director of Foreign Affairs, Rear Admiral Guan Youfei, spoke to selected reporters and called for the U.S. side to be "flexible" toward North Korea and spoke against sanctions to deal with its nuclear weapons program. At the DCT the next month, however, Under Secretary of Defense for Policy James Miller called on the PRC to maintain and increase pressure on North Korea to achieve denuclearization.

There is a challenge in engaging the PLA in comprehensive U.S. and international efforts to deal with the threat posed by North Korea's nuclear and missile programs. China hosted the first round of Six-Party Talks in August 2003 that also included Japan, South Korea, and Russia. The following month, PLA units replaced paramilitary People's Armed Police (PAP) units along China's border with North Korea, apparently to signal to Pyongyang the seriousness of the tensions and warn against provocative actions. China has stated a goal of a nuclear-free Korean peninsula and demonstrated its displeasure with North Korea after its missile and nuclear tests in 2006, including when CMC Vice Chairman Guo Boxiong visited Washington in 2006. However, China has shifted from pressuring North Korea with the military relationship to buttressing the DPRK regime's security and survival for stability. A related issue has arisen about how to discuss the PRC's military relationship with the DPRK, including any PLA contingency planning in the event of a crisis or collapse of the DPRK regime. Another issue concerns the challenge in talking with the PLA about contingencies that also could involve the U.S. and allied militaries. Other key questions concern the PLA's knowledge of the DPRK's missile and nuclear programs, plans to secure weapons and nuclear material, willingness to share intelligence with the United States and U.S. allies, and aim to exert control that could complicate U.S. and Republic of Korea (ROK) operations. The PLA has seen the DPRK as a "buffer," keeping U.S. and ROK forces below the 38th parallel. China supported the DPRK even after it attacked South Korea's naval ship and island in 2010. PLA General Ma Xiaotian, in July 2010, expressed "opposition" to even U.S.-ROK exercises in the Yellow Sea, in deterrence of the DPRK's belligerent threats.

Involving potential cooperation in nuclear nonproliferation, nuclear security, and counter-terrorism, the Departments of Energy and Defense agreed to establish a Center of Excellence on Nuclear Security in China during the visit of PRC leader Hu Jintao in January 2011. The PRC agency in implementing the agreement is the China Atomic Energy Authority (CAEA). One issue concerns compliance with restrictions in the FY2000 NDAA.

Strategic Nuclear, Missile, Space, and Cyber Talks

As for a strategic nuclear dialogue, the Clinton Administration had included nuclear forces as a priority area for expanded military discussions, including during the visits to China in 1998 of Secretary of Defense Cohen and President Clinton. In his visit to China in 1998, President

Clinton announced a bilateral "agreement" not to target strategic nuclear weapons against each other. However, the short statement was symbolic and lacked implementation.

Since then, concerns have increased about China's modernizing strategic nuclear force and its "No First Use" policy, including whether it is subject to debate. In July 2005, PLA Major General Zhu Chenghu, a dean at the PLA's National Defense University, told reporters in Beijing that "if the Americans draw their missiles and position-guided ammunition into the target zone on China's territory, I think we will have to respond with nuclear weapons," and he included the PLA's naval ships and fighters as China's "territory." Zhu added that if the United States is determined to intervene in a Taiwan scenario, "we will be determined to respond, and we Chinese will prepare ourselves for the destruction of all cities east of Xian [a city in north-central China]. Of course, the Americans will have to be prepared that hundreds of, or two hundreds of, or even more cities will be destroyed by the Chinese." Zhu also dismissed China's "No First Use" policy, saying that it applied only to non-nuclear states and could be changed. China's experts argued that Zhu's comments reflected China's concerns about the challenges presented by U.S. defense policy and nuclear strategy for China's policy.[106] Aside from such sensationalistic statements, the Defense Department's 2011 report to Congress on the PLA noted that "some PLA officers have written publicly of the need to spell out conditions under which China might need to use nuclear weapons first; for example, if an enemy's conventional attack threatened the survival of China's nuclear force, or of the regime itself. However, there has been no indication that national leaders are willing to attach such nuances and caveats to China's 'no first use' doctrine."

Moreover, there has been a challenge to engage with the Second Artillery. The PLA apparently views the Second Artillery as an operational unit with no role in discussions about nuclear policy and that China's nuclear deterrence rests partly on uncertainty. The PLA also has concerns about U.S. missile defense.[107] Still, when Secretary Rumsfeld visited China in October 2005, the PLA accorded him the honor of being the first foreigner to visit the Second Artillery's headquarters. Its commander, General Jing Zhiyuan, assured Rumsfeld that China would not be the first to use nuclear weapons.[108] General Jing later hosted the Chairman of the House Armed Services Committee, Representative Ike Skelton, at the Second Artillery's headquarters in August 2007.[109]

The Bush Administration invited General Jing to visit the Strategic Command (STRATCOM), as discussed during a summit between Presidents Bush and Hu Jintao in Washington in April 2006. Two months later, Assistant Secretary of Defense Peter Rodman visited Beijing for the DCT and discussed the invitation to the 2nd Artillery Commander. In October 2006, the STRATCOM commander, General James Cartwright (USMC), expressed interest in engaging with the PLA on space issues, including how the two sides could avoid and handle collisions or interference between satellites, and perceptions of attacks on satellites.[110] However, General Jing declined to schedule a visit.[111] On January 11, 2007, the PLA conducted its first successful direct ascent anti-

---

[106] Jason Dean, "Chinese General Lays Nuclear Card on U.S.' Table," *Wall Street Journal (WSJ)*, July 15, 2005; Danny Gittings, "General Zhu Goes Ballistic," *WSJ*, July 18, 2005; World Security Institute China Program, "Opening the Debate on U.S.-China Nuclear Relations," *China Security*, Autumn 2005.

[107] Author's consultation; and Jeremy Page, "U.S.-China Nuclear Silence Leaves a Void," *WSJ*, April 13, 2013.

[108] General Jing's reiteration of the "no first use" pledge was cited by one official PRC media report: "Rumsfeld Visits China; The Chinese Side Reiterates It Will Not Use Nuclear Weapons First," *Zhongguo Tongxun She [New China News Agency]*, October 20, 2005.

[109] *Xinhua* and *Associated Press*, August 27, 2007.

[110] Jeremy Singer, "Cartwright Seeks Closer Ties with China, Russia," *Space News*, October 16, 2006.

[111] Bill Gertz, "Chinese General's U.S. Visit for Nuke Talks Deferred," *Washington Times*, January 15, 2007.

---

satellite (ASAT) weapons test by launching a missile with a kinetic kill vehicle to destroy a PRC satellite.[112] (Later, in January 2010 and January 2013, the PLA carried out land-based mid-course missile interception tests. In May 2013, the PRC conducted another suspected ASAT test using a missile that reached over 6,200 miles above Earth). On June 13, 2007, Deputy Under Secretary of Defense Richard Lawless testified to the House Armed Services Committee that the PLA would not set a date to hold a dialogue on nuclear policy, strategy, and doctrine. Lawless said that PLA strategic forces have improved the capability to target the U.S. mainland.[113] The PLA's refusal raised questions about China's intentions and Hu Jintao's control over the PLA.

Still, the PRC reportedly has pursued ASAT programs for many years. The "Cox Committee" reported in 1999 that the PRC was believed to be developing space-based and ground-based ASAT laser weapons. The Departments of Defense and State reported in 2012 that China has improved its ability to track and identify satellites, a prerequisite for counter-space operations. The report told Congress that "the Departments are aware that some countries are pursuing advanced missile and space-related technologies for use against U.S. national interests. ... For example, China implements active and effective technology acquisition techniques that target U.S. space-related technologies and, therefore, warrants special scrutiny."[114]

The PLA took more modest steps in December 2007, when the PLA delegation to the 9th DCT included 2nd Artillery Deputy Chief of Staff Yang Zhiguo. In April 2008, the PLA and the Defense Department held talks on nuclear strategy at the "experts" level, indirectly involving the Defense Threat Reduction Agency (DTRA). The DTRA-sponsored Track 1.5 talks have continued. The PLA proposed to change the Pentagon-PLA defense policy talks into a "Strategic Dialogue," that would include nuclear policy. In early 2009, the National Security Council's Senior Director for Asia, Dennis Wilder, said that the PLA was intentionally being mysterious to have an advantage and expressed concerns about miscalculation and doubts China would engage in arms control.[115]

Under the Obama Administration, at a summit in Beijing in November 2009, President Obama repeated what President Clinton said about non-targeting of nuclear arms. In the first U.S.-PRC "Joint Statement" since 1997, Obama and Hu Jintao issued a "Joint Statement" which reaffirmed the U.S-PRC "commitment" of June 27, 1998, "not to target at each other the strategic nuclear weapons under their respective control." The two countries also claimed "common interests" in promoting the peaceful use of outer space.

While in India in January 2010, Secretary of Defense Robert Gates said that the United States sought to start a routine, in-depth dialogue with the PRC on strategic intentions and plans, in order to avoid miscalculations or misunderstandings and safeguard global stability. In April, Assistant Secretary of State for East Asian and Pacific Affairs Kurt Campbell also lamented that lagging behind a number of dialogues with the PRC has been the military dialogue, and lagging further beyond overall military talks has been a nuclear dialogue. The next month, Campbell said that the U.S. side proposed that Defense Department officials going to the S&ED in Beijing brief the PLA on the Quadrennial Defense Review (QDR) and Nuclear Posture Review (NPR) (of

---

[112] See CRS Report RS22652, *China's Anti-Satellite Weapon Test*, by Shirley A. Kan.

[113] House Armed Services Committee, hearing on "China: Recent Security Developments," June 13, 2007.

[114] House Select Committee on U.S. National Security and Military/Commercial Concerns with the People's Republic of China, unclassified report, May 1999; Departments of Defense and State, Report to Congress as Required by Section 1248 of the FY2010 NDAA (P.L. 111-84), Risk Assessment of United States Space Export Control Policy, April 2012.

[115] Quoted in "Bush Official Urges China to Lift Nuclear Secrecy," *AP*, January 14, 2009.

February and April 2010).[116] However, the PLA did not accept such DOD briefings on the agenda of the S&ED. The NPR called for a dialogue with China on "strategic stability"[117] to provide a mechanism for each side to communicate its views about the other's strategies, policies, and programs on nuclear weapons and other strategic capabilities, thereby enhancing confidence, improving transparency, and reducing mistrust. A model for U.S.-PLA discussion could be the PRC-Russian agreement of 2009, on mutual notifications of missile and space launches.

The Defense Secretary reported to Congress in August 2010 that after the first round of talks on nuclear policy and strategy in April 2008, the PLA has not agreed to further talks. Secretary Gates raised this concern with CMC Vice Chairman General Xu Caihou, when he visited in October 2009. General Chilton hosted General Xu for a brief visit at STRATCOM. Further, the report named as a priority a strategic dialogue in nuclear, space, and cybersecurity.

During his visit in early 2011, Secretary Gates again proposed a Strategic Dialogue and invited General Jing to visit. The PLA agreed to "study" the proposal. However, even before Gates met with Jing, the PLA issued a press statement to "sum up" Gates' visit. Moreover, the U.S.-PRC Joint Statement of January 19, 2011, issued at Hu Jintao's state visit did not note a "strategic dialogue" or a PLA visit to STRATCOM. Indeed, on April 27, the PLA's spokesman failed to acknowledge even consideration of a strategic dialogue or a visit by General Jing.

Still, at the 3rd S&ED on May 9-10, 2011, the Defense and State Departments started the first **Strategic Security Dialogue (SSD)** that brought together the PLA and the Foreign Ministry. The Defense Department contended that this SSD stemmed from Gates' proposal for strategic talks. The SSD discussed cyber and maritime disputes. Subsequently, the U.S. side faced a challenge in continuing the SSD outside the annual S&EDs. The Defense Secretary's 2011 report on the PLA told Congress that the PLA's writings have covered capabilities for cyber warfare.

Since the first SSD, the Defense Department issued, in July 2011, the first Strategy for Operating in Cyberspace. In the fall of 2011, the National Counterintelligence Executive (NCIX) submitted the first unclassified report to Congress since 2008 on economic espionage and the first to focus on cyber espionage. The NCIX reported that China's actors are the world's most active and persistent perpetrators of economic espionage and that there has been an onslaught of computer network intrusions that originated in China, though that report claimed an inability to confirm the attackers. However, a private research organization reported on the PLA's suspected cyber organizations. A later news report stressed that the National Security Agency (NSA) indeed has tracked cyber threats to groups connected to the PLA and that such attacks have targeted U.S. defense programs. A former Director of National Intelligence (DNI), Secretary of Homeland Security, and Deputy Secretary of Defense wrote that the PRC has a national policy of economic espionage in cyberspace.[118] The PACOM Commander, Admiral Robert Willard, testified to the

---

[116] Department of Defense, "Press Conference with Secretary Gates from India," January 20, 2010; "China and Nuclear Talks," *Washington Times*, April 29, 2010; State Department, "Briefing on the Upcoming U.S.-China Strategic and Economic Dialogue," May 19, 2010.

[117] On "strategic stability," see, for example: Brad Roberts, "Strategic Deterrence Beyond Taiwan," in *Beyond the Strait: PLA Missions Other Than Taiwan* (Army War College, April 2009); Li Bin and Nie Hongzhen, "An Investigation of China-U.S. Strategic Stability," Union of Concerned Scientists, May 2009; M. Taylor Fravel and Evan Medeiros, "China's Search for Assured Retaliation," *International Security*, Fall 2010; Dean Cheng, "Chinese Views on Deterrence," *Joint Forces Quarterly*, 1st Quarter 2011; Lora Saalman, "China and the U.S. Nuclear Posture Review," Carnegie-Tsinghua Center for Global Policy, February 2011; Christopher Castelli, "Draft Report Urges Accepting Mutual Nuclear Vulnerability With China," *Inside Defense*, July 25, 2012.

[118] NCIX, "Foreign Spies Stealing U.S. Economic Secrets in Cyberspace," October 2011; Mark Stokes, Jenny Lin, (continued...)

Senate Armed Services Committee on February 28, 2012, that China's active development of cyber and space capabilities fell within its military modernization. In May, visiting Defense Minister Liang Guanglie denied that cyber intrusions originate from China but offered to talk about cybersecurity. U.S. officials cited cyber activities that appeared to originate in China.

Members of Congress have raised concerns about China's use of cyber espionage to advance the PLA's power as well as the economy's growth. In May 2012, the Defense Department's annual report on the PLA reported to Congress that PRC telecommunications companies, such as Huawei, Datang, and Zhongxing (ZTE), have ties to the PRC government and PLA entities. Moreover, on October 8, after an investigation and hearing, the House Intelligence Committee warned of risks to U.S. national security from using Huawei or ZTE products. The next day, the State Department's spokesperson confirmed that concerns were raised at the SSD about cyber threats. Days later, Defense Secretary Panetta warned in a speech about a "cyber Pearl Harbor." He said he raised concerns when he was in Beijing in September about communication and transparency to avoid miscalculation or misunderstanding about advanced cyber capabilities.[119]

On February 18, 2013, a private firm, Mandiant, issued a report that pointed to cyber threats from the PLA's **Unit 61398** in Shanghai (the 2nd Bureau of the 3rd Department of the GSD). The next day, the State Department's spokesperson confirmed that the Administration raised at the highest level the substantial and growing concerns about China's cyber threats to U.S. economic and security interests that involved the PLA. At the same time, the Administration reportedly and quietly provided Internet service providers the suspected Internet Protocol addresses linked to the PLA unit to protect U.S. networks from malicious cyber activity.[120] However, at the end of February, the PLA's spokesperson criticized Mandiant's report as unprofessional and not factual, insisted that PRC law prohibits cyber "attacks," denied that the PLA supported hacking, and called China a victim of cyber "attacks." Still, the PLA's spokesperson did not deny the alleged activities of Unit 61398, saying that he could not reveal the secret missions of specific units.

The Administration has shifted to raise concerns about cyber threats with the PRC publicly and at a higher level, including threats against national networks and critical infrastructure. National Security Advisor Tom Donilon said in a speech on March 11 that concerns about cyber threats, not ordinary cyber crime or hacking, moved to the forefront of the agenda with China (up to the level of the President). The next day, DNI James Clapper presented an assessment of worldwide threats to the Senate Select Committee on Intelligence, stressing cyber threats before other global threats to the United States and calling China and Russia "advanced cyber actors." In a phone call with top PRC leader Xi Jinping on March 14, President Obama raised cyber threats as a "shared challenge." In May, the Secretary of Defense's annual report on the PLA told Congress that there

---

(...continued)

Russell Hsiao, "The Chinese People's Liberation Army Signals Intelligence and Cyber Reconnaissance Infrastructure," Project 2049 Institute, November 11, 2011; Siobhan Gorman, "U.S. Homes in On China Spying," *Wall Street Journal*, December 13, 2011; Mike McConnell, Michael Chertoff, William Lynn, "China's Cyber Thievery is National Policy– And Must be Challenged," *Wall Street Journal*, January 27, 2012.

[119] Representatives Mike Rogers and Dutch Ruppersberger, chairman and ranking Member of the House Intelligence Committee, "China's Cyber Trade War Against the U.S.," *Politico*, April 26, 2012, and "Investigative Report on the U.S. National Security Issues Posed by Chinese Telecommunications Companies Huawei and ZTE," October 8, 2012; Defense Department, "Remarks by Secretary Panetta on Cybersecurity to the Business Executives for National Security," New York City, October 11, 2012.

[120] Mandiant, "APT1: Exposing One of China's Cyber Espionage Units," February 18, 2013; Danny Yadron and Siobhan Gorman, "U.S., Firms Draw a Bead on Chinese Cyberspies," *Wall Street Journal*, July 12, 2013.

were some cyber intrusions in 2012 against U.S. government computer systems that were attributable directly to the PRC government and PLA. The report also noted the PLA's use of cyberwarfare. At the Shangri-la Dialogue in June, Secretary of Defense Chuck Hagel expressed U.S. concerns about the growing threat of cyber intrusions, including from the PLA. However, some skeptics, such as former Secretary of Homeland Security Michael Chertoff, warned that diplomacy would not end China's cyber threats. Others argued that China's sense of its own vulnerabilities in nuclear, space, and cyber domains could result in mutual restraint.[121]

The PRC shifted slightly in public from outright denials, counter-accusations, conflating various cyber activities, rejection of laws of warfare in cyberspace, promotion of sovereign control over cyberspace, and expressions of victimization to a stance of some willingness to talk about cooperation in cybersecurity. In April 2013, Secretary of State John Kerry announced in Beijing that the PRC agreed to a new Working Group on Cybersecurity. In his visit to Beijing, the Chairman of the Joint Chiefs of Staff, General Dempsey, urged collaboration and transparency since both countries have strong economies, rely on technology, and share cyber vulnerabilities. At the summit with Xi at Sunnylands Retreat, CA, on June 8, President Obama asserted that they both recognize the need for international rules and common approaches to cybersecurity in the bilateral relationship, and Xi said that cybersecurity could be a positive area of cooperation.

However, the next day, complications arose with Edward Snowden's revelations of his presence in Hong Kong and allegations of NSA surveillance of computer systems, including in Hong Kong and China. In an interview on *PBS* on June 17, President Obama distinguished between common intelligence collection by many governments versus the PRC government's or the PLA's cyber-enabled theft against U.S. companies. On June 23, Hong Kong allowed Snowden to fly to Moscow. Moreover, China used Snowden's case to protest to the United States about conflated "cyber attacks," despite the PRC's suspected surveillance against its own citizens (especially resulting in reported monitoring of Tibetans and imprisonment of Uighurs for their allegedly illegal Internet activities). The next day, the White House warned that the deliberate decision to release the U.S. fugitive presented a negative impact on the U.S.-China relationship.

Still, in July 2013, both sides held another S&ED, and U.S. and PRC civilian and military officials held the first meeting of the Cyber Working Group under the SSD on July 8. Both sides agreed to talk more about international cyber norms and principles. President Obama reiterated U.S. concerns about cyber-enabled theft of trade secrets to Vice Premier Wang Yang and State Councilor Yang Jiechi. President Obama also expressed disappointment and concern with how the PRC handled Snowden's case. Defense Secretary Hagel stressed to Yang the need to cooperate in cyberspace, but PRC official media did not mention any remarks on cyber security by Yang to Hagel. The Cyber Working Group held a second meeting on December 3, 2013, in Beijing.

Even after those meetings and before the Justice Department's indictments against PLA hackers, the PLA spokesman, on March 27, 2014, charged U.S. "hypocrisy" with no mention of cooperation. In early 2014, the Defense Department, reportedly worried about potential escalations in cyber attacks and counter attacks, briefed the PLA for the first time on the U.S. doctrine for cyber capabilities, but the PLA did not reciprocate with its briefing. In Beijing in April, Defense Secretary Hagel said the U.S. side has been more open about cyber capabilities,

---

[121] Interview with Michael Chertoff, *Defense News*, March 11, 2013; David Gompert and Philip Saunders, "Sino-American Strategic Restraint in an Age of Vulnerability," *Strategic Forum*, National Defense University, January 2012.

including an "approach of restraint," and has urged China to brief in return.[122] On May 19, Attorney General Eric Holder announced indictments against five hackers of the PLA's Unit 61398 for economic espionage through cyber theft to steal trade secrets of U.S. companies for commercial advantage from 2006 to 2014. Thus, the PLA's cyber theft continued despite the Working Group. The PRC suspended the Cyber Working Group after the indictments. On June 9, a cyber security company, CrowdStrike, reported that another group of hackers has worked in the PLA's **Unit 61486** (12th Bureau of the 3rd Department of the GSD) in Shanghai.[123]

Counterterrorism

The PRC's cooperation in counterterrorism after the attacks on September 11, 2001, has not included military cooperation with the U.S. military. The U.S. Commanders of the Central and Pacific Commands, General Tommy Franks and Admiral Dennis Blair, separately confirmed in April 2002 that the PLA did not provide cooperation (nor was it requested) in Operation Enduring Freedom against Al Qaeda in Afghanistan (e.g., basing, staging, or overflight) and that China's shared intelligence was not specific enough. Also, the Pentagon issued a report in June 2002 on the international coalition fighting terrorism and did not include China among the countries providing military contributions. China has provided diplomatic support, cited by the State Department. U.S.-PRC counterterrorism cooperation has been limited, while U.S. concerns have increased about the PRC's increased influence in the Shanghai Cooperation Organization (SCO) and its call for U.S. withdrawals from Central Asia, and about PRC-origin small arms and anti-aircraft missiles found in Afghanistan and Iraq.[124]

Some have urged caution in military cooperation with China on this front, while others see benefits for the U.S. relationship with China and the war on terrorism. Senator Bob Smith and Representative Dana Rohrabacher wrote Secretary of Defense Rumsfeld in late 2001, to express concerns about renewed military contacts with China. In part, they argued that "China is not a good prospect for counterterrorism cooperation," because of concerns that China has practiced internal repression in the name of counterterrorism and has supplied technology to rogue regimes and state sponsors of terrorism.[125] In contrast, a report by Rand in 2004 urged a program of security management with China that includes counterterrorism as one of three components.[126]

As preparations intensified for the summer Olympic Games in Beijing in 2008, a policy issue concerned the extent to which the United States, including the U.S. military, should support security at the games to protect U.S. citizens and should cooperate with the PLA and the paramilitary PAP. With concerns about internal repression by the PRC regime in the Tiananmen Crackdown of June 1989 and after, U.S. sanctions (in §902 of the Foreign Relations Authorization Act for FY1990-FY1991, P.L. 101-246) have denied the export to China of defense articles/services, including helicopters, as well as crime control equipment. Presidential waivers are authorized. A precedent was set in 2004, when various U.S. departments, including the Department of Defense, provided security assistance for the Olympic Games in Athens, Greece,

---

[122] David Sanger, "U.S. Tries Candor to Assure China on Cyberattacks," *New York Times*, April 6, 2014; Defense Department, Remarks by Secretary Hagel, PLA NDU, Beijing, April 8, 2014.

[123] CrowdStrike, "Putter Panda," June 9, 2014; *New York Times*, June 9, 2014.

[124] See CRS Report RL33001, *U.S.-China Counterterrorism Cooperation: Issues for U.S. Policy*, by Shirley A. Kan.

[125] Bob Smith and Dana Rohrabacher, letter to Secretary of Defense Donald Rumsfeld, December 17, 2001.

[126] Rand, "U.S.-China Security Management: Assessing the Military-to-Military Relationship," July 2004.

in 2004. On June 22, 2006, at a hearing of the House Armed Services Committee, Brigadier General John Allen, the Principal Director for Asian and Pacific Affairs at the Office of the Secretary of Defense, testified that the Pentagon started discussions with China regarding security cooperation for the 2008 Olympics. However, Deputy Under Secretary of Defense Richard Lawless testified to the House Armed Services Committee on June 13, 2007, that China did not accept offers from the Defense Department to assist in Olympic security.

In February 2009, U.S. policymakers proposed a non-lethal supply route from China to Afghanistan, partly due to worry about the vulnerable route through Pakistan. The proposal did not see progress, but seemed less urgent after Kyrgyzstan in June reversed its threat in February to evict U.S. forces from Manas air base. Speaking at the annual Shangri-la Dialogue in Singapore in May 2009, Defense Secretary Gates said that he would welcome China's help in Afghanistan, including for security assistance of civilian efforts there.[127]

Any military cooperation with China would involve stark differences on human rights. The United States takes into account the role of the PRC's armed forces, including the paramilitary PAP, in internal security (including against Tibetan and Uighur peoples in the western regions). After an earthquake in Port-Au-Prince, Haiti, in January 2010, the Army's 82nd Airborne had soldiers conduct the first U.S. combined patrol with U.N. peacekeepers there. However, the U.N. unit was a PAP unit deployed in police uniforms of the Ministry of Public Security (MPS).[128]

Accounting for POW/MIAs

For humanitarian reasons or to advance the broader U.S.-PRC relationship, the PLA has been helpful in U.S. efforts to resolve POW/MIA cases from World War II, the Vietnam War, and the Cold War. In February 2001, the Defense Department characterized PRC assistance to the United States in recovering remains from World War II as "generous," citing the missions in 1994 in Tibet and in 1997-1999 in Maoer Mountain in southern China.[129]

However, for 16 years—even as the survivors of those lost in the Korean War were aging and dying—the United States faced a challenge in securing the PLA's cooperation in U.S. accounting for POW/MIAs from the Korean War. Despite visits by the Director of the Defense POW/MIA Office (DPMO) and other military officials to China and improved bilateral relations, the United States was not able to announce progress in obtaining cooperation from the PLA until 2008.

In April 1992, a military official in Eastern Europe supplied a report to then Secretary of Defense Dick Cheney, alleging that "several dozen" American military personnel captured in the Korean War (1950-1953) were sent to a camp in the Northeastern city of Harbin in China where they were used in psychological and medical experiments before being executed or dying in captivity.[130] In May 1992, the State Department raised the issue of POW/MIAs with the PRC, saying it was a "matter of the highest national priority," and in June 1992, the Senate Select Committee on POW/MIA Affairs received information from the Russian government indicating that over 100 American POWs captured in the Korean War were interrogated by the Soviet Union

---

[127] Vijay Joshi, "U.S. Urges Europe, China to Step up Afghan Help," *AP*, May 30, 2009.

[128] "China, U.S. Peacekeepers Conduct Joint Patrol in Haiti," *Xinhua*, January 29, 2010. Dennis Blasko, ex-Army Attache, noted that this MPS unit belonged to the PAP Yunnan Border Defense unit and may wear MPS uniforms.

[129] Department of Defense, news release, "China Provides World War II U.S. Aircraft Crash Sites," February 8, 2001.

[130] Melissa Healy, "China Said to Have Experimented on U.S. POWs," *Los Angeles Times*, July 4, 1992.

and possibly sent to China.[131] The United States also presented to the PRC a list of 125 American military personnel still unaccounted for since the Korean War, who were believed to have been interrogated in the Soviet Union and then sent to China. China responded to the United States that it did not receive anyone on that list from the former Soviet Union.[132] But that response apparently did not address whether China received American military personnel from North Korea or China itself transferred them.

Upon returning from North Korea and Southeast Asia in December 1992, Senator Robert Smith, Vice Chairman of the Select Committee on POW/MIA Affairs, disclosed that officials in Pyongyang admitted that "hundreds" of American POWs captured in the Korean War were sent to China and did not return to North Korea. According to Smith, North Korean officials said that China's PLA operated POW camps in North Korea during the Korean War and the Cold War and detained Americans in China's northeastern region. Moreover, North Korean officials told Smith that some American POWs could have been sent to the Soviet Union for further interrogations. Smith advocated that the U.S. government press the PRC government for information on POWs rather than accept the PRC's denials that it had POWs or information about them, saying "this is where the answers lie."[133] (The Senate created the Select Committee on POW/MIA Affairs in August 1991, chaired by Senator John Kerry. It concluded in December 1992, after gaining "important new information" from North Korea on China's involvement with U.S. POWs.)[134]

Secretary of Defense Cohen visited China in 1998 and stressed cooperation on POW/MIA cases one of four priorities in exchanges with the PLA. After visiting China in January 1999 to seek the PLA's cooperation in opening its secret archives on the Korean War, the Director of DPMO, Robert Jones, said that "we believe that Chinese records of the war may hold the key to resolving the fates of many of our missing servicemen from the Korean War." DPMO's spokesman, Larry Greer, reported that the PRC agreed to look into the U.S. request to access the archives.[135]

In March 2003, DPMO Director Jerry Jennings visited China and said that PRC records likely hold "the key" to resolving some POW/MIA cases from the Korean War.[136] Just days after the Chairman of the Joint Chiefs of Staff, General Myers, visited Beijing in January 2004, PRC media reported on January 19, 2004, that the government declassified the first batch of over 10,000 files in its archives on the PRC's foreign relations from 1949 to 1955. However, this step apparently excluded wartime records, and General Myers did not announce cooperation by China in providing information in its archives related to American POW/MIAs from the Korean War.[137] The PRC later announced in July 2004 the declassification of a second batch of similar files. In February 2005, DPMO acknowledged that PRC cooperation on Korean War cases remained the "greatest challenge."[138]

---

[131] Mark Sauter, "POW Probe Extends to Korea, China," *Tacoma News-Tribune*, June 21, 1992.

[132] "No U.S. POWs in China," *Beijing Review*, July 27-August 2, 1992.

[133] Carleton R. Bryant, "N. Korea: POWs Sent to China: Senator Says U.S. Must Prod Beijing," *Washington Times*, December 23, 1992.

[134] Report of the Select Committee on POW/MIA Affairs, S.Rept. 103-1, January 3, 1993.

[135] Sue Pleming, "U.S. Asks China for Access to Korean POW Files," *Reuters*, February 4, 1999.

[136] Department of Defense, "U.S., China Agree to Enhanced Cooperation on POW/MIA Matters," March 29, 2003.

[137] Author's consultation with DPMO, January 29, 2004.

[138] DPMO, "Personnel Accounting Progress in China as of February 4, 2005," February 2005.

Visiting Beijing with Defense Secretary Donald Rumsfeld in October 2005, Pentagon officials again raised the issue of access to China's Korean War archives believed to hold documents on American POWs.[139] In July 2006, General Guo Boxiong (the top PLA officer) visited the United States and agreed to open PLA archives on the Korean War. However, in his June 2007 report to Congress on military contacts, Secretary Gates reported that the PLA's help "yielded mixed results." PLA cooperation with DPMO was "limited" in 2006, despite General Guo's promise.

There was some progress in February 2008, when China finally agreed to allow access to the PLA archives on the Korean War. However, the PLA did not grant direct U.S. access to the records, as asked by the Defense Department. The DPMO would have to request searches done by PRC researchers at the archives, and the PLA would control and turn over deemed acceptable records. The two sides also had to negotiate the frequency, amount, and expenses of the PLA's searches. Deputy Assistant Secretary of Defense for POW/MIA Affairs Charles Ray signed an initial Memorandum in Shanghai on February 29, 2008, which was followed by a detailed memorandum on April 24, 2008.[140] Despite the PRC's refusal to cooperate for many years, a PRC Foreign Ministry spokesman claimed China agreed out of "humanitarianism."[141] The United States also has had a challenge in seeking information on POW camps run by the PLA in North Korea.

DPMO agreed to pay the PLA for its research in the amount of $75,000 semi-annually, at no more than $150,000 each fiscal year. Under the agreed arrangement, the two sides have held annual meetings in the United States and the PRC, and the PLA has provided progress reports and annual reports. On July 10, 2008, the House Armed Services Subcommittee on Military Personnel held a hearing on POWs and MIAs, with discussion of POW/MIAs taken to China during the Korean War, including Sergeant Richard Desautels who was buried in China in 1953. In mid-2009, the PLA finally provided to the DOD initial information, but that report consisted of 25 pages of summaries of supposedly classified documents on U.S. POW/MIAs from the Korean War (and not the documents), after the United States paid the PLA $150,000.[142] Still, DPMO has gotten some progress from the PLA in its willingness over cooperation since 2008. During CMC Vice Chairman General Xu Caihou's visit in October 2009, he provided information to Defense Secretary Gates about a site in Guangdong province where a U.S. aircraft crashed, part of new insights for the Defense Department which had thought the plane crashed into the sea. The PLA also provided new information on five cases of aircraft that crashed in China and North Korea. The PLA Archives Department provided its second annual report in 2010, but there was a gap of five months (April-September 2009) between the first and second reports. The DPMO has continued to rely on the PLA's reporting of its archival research, with a third written report

---

[139] Robert Burns, "Pentagon Seeking Access to Chinese Records on War MIAs," *AP/Arizona Republic*, October 23, 2005; and author's discussions with DPMO.

[140] "Pentagon Cites MIA Deal With China," *AP*, February 25, 2008, quoting DPMO spokesman Larry Greer; and Defense Department, "U.S. and China Sign POW/ MIA Arrangement," news release, February 29, 2008. DPMO signed two memoranda with the PLA and its Archives Department: "Memorandum of Arrangement Between the Department of Defense, the United States of America, and the Ministry of National Defense, the People's Republic of China, to Establish and Develop Military Archives Cooperation Activities to Search for Information Relating to U.S. Military Personnel Missing in Action Before, During, and After the Korean War," February 29, 2008; and "Memorandum of Arrangement on Developing Military Archive Cooperation Between the U.S. Department of Defense Prisoner of War/Missing Personnel Office and the People's Liberation Army Archives Department on Information Relating to U.S. Military Personnel Missing in Action Before, During, and After the Korean War," April 24, 2008.

[141] "PRC Will Continually Help Look for Remains of U.S. Soldiers Killed in Korean War," *Xinhua*, February 28, 2008.

[142] "Inside the Ring," *Washington Times*, July 16, 2009; PLA Archives Department, "Achievement Document of Military Archives Cooperation Between the People's Republic of China and the United States of America, October 2008 – April 2009."

---

submitted to the U.S. side in September 2011, again for $150,000, but with no meeting.[143] The Memorandum signed in April 2008 expired in April 2011 and required a revised agreement. The DPMO signed a new technical arrangement on May 17, 2012, for a period until May 16, 2015. The arrangement agreed to the same amount of $150,000 per year and expanded coverage of the PLA's archival research to include World War II, Cold War, and Vietnam War. The DPMO still would not have direct access to the archive.

---

[143] DPMO, "Personnel Accounting Progress in China," September 30, 2011; PLA Archives Department, "The Achievement Document of Military Archives Cooperation Between the People's Republic of China and the United States of America, September 2009-August 2010"; and report for August 2010-August 2011.

Appendix. Major Military Contacts and Incidents Since 1993

The scope of this record of mil-to-mil contacts focuses on senior-level visits, strategic talks, functional exchanges, agreements, commissions, and training or exercises. This compiled record does not provide a detailed list of all mil-to-mil contacts (that also include confidence building measures (CBMs), educational exchanges that include visits by students at U.S. military colleges and the Capstone educational program for new U.S. general/flag officers, the numerous port visits in Hong Kong that continued after its hand-over from British to PRC control in July 1997, disaster relief missions, and multilateral conferences). There is no security assistance, as U.S. sanctions against arms sales have remained since 1989. Sources include numerous official statements, reports to Congress, documents, news stories, consultations, and observations. Specific dates are provided to the extent possible, while there are instances in which just the month is reported. Text boxes summarize major bilateral tensions in crises or confrontations as a context for the alternating periods of enthusiastic and skeptical contacts.

1993

> In July 1993, the Clinton Administration suspected that a PRC cargo ship, called the *Yinhe*, was going to Iran with chemicals that could be used for chemical weapons and sought to inspect its cargo. In an unusual move, on August 9, China first disclosed that it protested U.S. "harassment" and finally allowed U.S. participation in a Saudi inspection of the ship's cargo on August 26, 1993. Afterward, the State Department said that the suspected chemicals were not found on the ship at that time. The PRC has raised this Yinhe incident as a grievance against the United States and the credibility of U.S. intelligence in particular.

November 1-2	Assistant Secretary of Defense for International Security Affairs Chas Freeman visited to renew mil-to-mil ties for the first time since the Tiananmen Crackdown in June 1989. Freeman met with General Liu Huaqing (a CMC Vice Chairman), General Chi Haotian (Defense Minister), LTG Xu Huizi (a Deputy Chief of General Staff), and LTG Huai Guomo (Vice Chairman of COSTIND).

1994

January 17-21	LTG Paul Cerjan, President of NDU, visited China to advance professional military exchanges with the PLA's NDU. Cerjan visited the Nanjing MR and saw the 179th Infantry Division.
March 11-14	Under Secretary of Defense for Policy Frank Wisner visited China, along with Secretary of State Warren Christopher.
July 6-8	PACOM Commander Admiral Charles Larson visited China and held talks with PLA Deputy Chief of General Staff, General Xu Huizi.
August 15-18	The Director of the PRC's National Bureau of Surveying and Mapping (NBSM) visited the United States and signed an agreement for a cooperative program with the Defense Mapping Agency, the predecessor of the National Imagery and Mapping Agency (NIMA), regarding the global positioning system (GPS). The agreement refers to the "Protocol for Scientific and Technical Cooperation in Surveying and Mapping Studies Concerning Scientific and Technical Cooperation in the Application of Geodetic and Geophysical Data to Mapping, Charting, and Geodetic (MC&G) Programs."
August 15-25	Deputy Chief of General Staff, General Xu Huizi, visited the United States and met with Defense Secretary William Perry and General John Shalikashvili, Chairman of the Joint Chiefs of Staff, in Washington, DC, and PACOM Commander, Admiral Richard Macke, in Hawaii.

September 7-29	In a POW/MIA operation, a U.S. Army team traveled to Tibet with PLA support to recover the remains of two U.S. airmen whose C-87 cargo plane crashed into a glacier at 14,000 feet in Tibet on December 31, 1944, during a flight over the "hump" back to India from Kunming, China, in World War II.
September 19-24	Chief of Staff of the U.S. Air Force, General Merrill McPeak, visited China and met with PLA Air Force Commander, General Cao Shuangming.
October 16-19	Secretary of Defense William Perry visited China and met with Generals Liu Huaqing (CMC Vice Chairman) and Chi Haotian (Defense Minister). On October 17, Perry and PLA General Ding Henggao, Director of COSTIND, conducted the first meeting of the newly-established U.S.-China Joint Defense Conversion Commission. They signed the "U.S.-China Joint Defense Conversion Commission: Minutes of the First Meeting, Beijing, October 17, 1994."

In a confrontation in the Yellow Sea on October 27-29, 1994, the U.S. aircraft carrier battle group led by the USS *Kitty Hawk* discovered and tracked a Han-class nuclear attack submarine of the PLA Navy. In response, the PLA Air Force sent fighters toward the U.S. S-3 Viking aircraft tracking the submarine. Although no shots were fired by either side, China followed up the incident with a warning, issued to the U.S. Naval Attache over dinner in Beijing, that the PLA would open fire in a future incident.

November 5-10	The Director of the Defense Intelligence Agency (DIA), LTG James Clapper, visited China. He met with the GSD's Second Department (Intelligence) and the affiliated China Institute for International Strategic Studies (CIISS), saw the 179th Division in Nanjing, and received a briefing on tactical intelligence.
November 11-15	The Administrator of the Federal Aviation Administration, David Hinson, and the Defense Department's Executive Director of the Policy Board on Federal Aviation, Frank Colson, visited China to formulate the "U.S.-China 8-Step Civil-Military Air Traffic Control Cooperative Plan" agreed to during establishment of the Joint Defense Conversion Commission.
November 19-26	The PLA sent a delegation of new general and flag officers to the United States (similar to the U.S. Capstone program), led by LTG Ma Weizhi, Vice President of the NDU. They visited: Fort Irwin (National Training Center); Nellis Air Force Base (observed a Red Flag exercise); Washington, DC (for meetings at NDU and Pentagon, including with the Vice Chairman of the Joint Chiefs of Staff, Admiral William Owens); and Norfolk Naval Base (and toured an aircraft carrier).
December	A delegation from NIMA visited China to sign a GPS survey plan and discuss provision of PRC data on gravity for a NIMA/NASA project on gravity modeling and establishment of a GPS tracking station near Beijing.
December 10-13	Assistant Secretary of Defense for Strategy and Requirements Ted Warner visited China to brief on the U.S. defense strategy and budget as part of a defense transparency initiative, based on an agreement between Secretary Perry and General Chi Haotian in October 1994.

1995

| January 28-February 10 | PLA Major General Wen Guangchun, Assistant to the Director of the General Logistics Department (GLD), visited at the invitation of the Office of the Under Secretary of Defense for Acquisition and Technology. The U.S. military briefed on logistics doctrine and systems and allowed the PLA visitors to observe U.S. military logistics activities and installations. |
| February 6-10 | U.S. Air Force Deputy Chief of Staff for Plans and Operations, LTG Joseph Ralston, led a delegation from the Departments of Defense and Commerce, and Federal Aviation Administration. They discussed the PRC's military-civil air traffic control system and cooperation. |

In early February 1995, the PLA Navy occupied Mischief Reef in the Spratly Islands in the South China Sea, although Mischief Reef is about 150 miles west of the Philippines' island of Palawan but over 620 miles southeast of China's Hainan Island off its southern coast. China seized a claim to territory in the South China Sea against a country other than Vietnam for the first time and challenged the Philippines, a U.S. treaty ally. Some Members of Congress introduced resolutions urging U.S. support for peace and stability. Three months later, on May 10, 1995, the Clinton Administration issued a statement opposing the use or threat of force to resolve the competing claims, without naming China.

February 24-March 7	President of the PLA's NDU, LTG Zhu Dunfa, visited West Point in New York; NDU and Pentagon in Washington, DC; Maxwell Air Force Base in Alabama; Naval Air Station North Island (and boarded an Aegis-equipped cruiser), Marine Recruit Depot, and Camp Pendleton Marine Corps Base in California; and PACOM in Hawaii.
March 22-24	The USS *Bunker Hill* (Aegis-equipped, Ticonderoga-class cruiser) visited Qingdao, in the first U.S. Navy ship visit to China since 1989. The senior officer aboard, Rear Admiral Bernard Smith, Commander of Carrier Group Five, met with Vice Admiral Wang Jiying, Commander of the PLA Navy (PLAN)'s North Sea Fleet.
March 25-28	A Deputy Director of COSTIND, LTG Huai Guomo, visited Washington to meet with officials at the Department of Commerce, Department of Defense, and people in the private sector to discuss possible projects for the Joint Defense Conversion Commission.
March 26-April 2	LTG Xiong Guangkai, PLA Assistant Chief of General Staff (with the portfolio of military intelligence), visited the United States, reciprocating for Assistant Secretary of Defense for Strategy and Requirements Ted Warner's visit to Beijing in December 1994. Xiong provided briefings on the PLA's defense strategy and budget, and the composition of the armed forces, and received briefings on U.S. national and global information infrastructures.
March 28-April 4	A delegation from the PRC's National Bureau of Surveying and Mapping visited the United States to hold discussions with NIMA and release PRC gravity data for analysis.
April 19	Vice Minister of the General Administration of Civil Aviation (CAAC) Bao Peide visited the United States to meet with the Federal Aviation Administration and U.S. companies. U.S. Air Force Deputy Chief of Staff for Plans and Operations, Lieutenant General Ralph Eberhart, briefed the PRC delegation on U.S. Air Force air traffic control programs.
April 25-30	PACOM Commander, Admiral Richard Macke, visited China, hosted by PLA Deputy Chief of General Staff, General Xu Huizi.
May 17-22	PLA Air Force Commander, Lieutenant General Yu Zhenwu, visited the United States, hosted by the U.S. Air Force Chief of Staff. Originally scheduled to last until May 27, the PLA ended the visit on May 22 to protest the Clinton Administration's decision to grant a visa to Taiwan's President Lee Teng-hui to visit his alma mater, Cornell University.

On July 21-28, 1995, after the Clinton Administration allowed Taiwan's President Lee Teng-hui to make a private visit to give a speech at Cornell University on June 9, the PLA launched M-9 short-range ballistic missiles in "test-firings" toward target areas in the East China Sea. The PLA held other exercises directed against Taiwan until November.

On August 3, 1995, China expelled two U.S. Air Force attaches stationed in Hong Kong who were detained in China. China accused them of collecting military intelligence in restricted military areas along the southeastern coast.

August 31-September 2	PLA Commander of the Guangzhou MR, LTG Li Xilin, visited Hawaii to commemorate the 50th anniversary of victory in the Pacific in WWII. Li met with Secretary of Defense Perry, Chairman of the Joint Chiefs of Staff, General Shalikashvili, and PACOM Commander, Admiral Macke.
September 7-16	Two NIMA teams visited China to establish GPS satellite tracking stations and discuss plans for a GPS survey in China in 1996.

October 15-25	Lieutenant General (USAF) Ervin Rokke, President of the NDU, visited China and held talks with LTG Xing Shizhong, President of the PLA's NDU, about military educational exchanges. The PLA arranged for Rokke to visit the 196th Infantry Division under the Beijing MR, the Satellite Control Center in Xian (the first U.S. access), the Guilin Army Academy in Guilin, and the Guangzhou MR.
November 14-18	Assistant Secretary of Defense for International Security Affairs Joseph Nye visited Beijing and met with General Chi Haotian. Nye said that "nobody knows" what the United States would do if the PLA attacked Taiwan.

1996

On January 19, 1996, China expelled the U.S. Assistant Air Force Attache and the Japanese Air Force Attache, after detaining them while they were traveling in southern China.

January 20-27	Deputy Chief of Staff for Plans and Operations of the U.S. Air Force, Lieutenant General Ralph Eberhart, visited China with a delegation from the Departments of Defense and Commerce, and Federal Aviation Administration for the Air Traffic Control Cooperative Program.
January 31-February 4	The USS *Fort McHenry*, a dock-landing ship, visited Shanghai, under the command of Rear Admiral Walter Doran.
February 6	Visiting PRC Vice Foreign Minister Li Zhaoxing met with Under Secretary of Defense for Policy Walter Slocombe at the Pentagon.
March 7	Secretary of Defense Perry, along with National Security Advisor Anthony Lake, attended a dinner meeting hosted by Secretary of State Christopher at the State Department for PRC Foreign Affairs Office Director Liu Huaqiu. Perry warned Liu that there would be "grave consequences" should the PLA attack Taiwan.

On March 8-15, 1996, the PLA launched four M-9 short-range ballistic missiles into waters close to the two ports of Keelung and Kaohsiung in Taiwan. Leading up to Taiwan's first democratic presidential election on March 23, the PLA conducted live fire exercises in the Taiwan Strait on March 12-25. Neither U.S. nor Taiwan forces could counter a coercive use of ballistic missiles. The U.S. Navy sent the Aegis-equipped cruiser, USS *Bunker Hill*, to track the missiles, according to "Ready for Sea: Ballistic Missile Defense Study Findings on Navy Theater Wide TBMD (1994-1998)."

On March 10-11, 1996, the United States announced the deployment of two aircraft carriers, the USS *Independence* and USS *Nimitz*, to waters near the east coast of Taiwan.

March 9-17	Assistant Secretary of Defense for Health Affairs Stephen Joseph visited China to advance bilateral military medical relations. Joseph and a Deputy Director of the GLD, LTG Zhou Youliang, signed a "Memorandum of Medical Exchange and Cooperation."
April 5-13	Geodesy and geophysical staff from NIMA visited China to hold discussions with the PRC's National Bureau of Surveying and Mapping.
May 4-20	A geodesy and geophysical survey team from NIMA visited China to perform a cooperative GPS survey.
June 25-28	Under Secretary of Defense for Policy Walter Slocombe visited China.
July 11-August 31	The PRC's National Bureau of Surveying and Mapping visited the United States to hold discussions with NIMA on cooperative projects and computation of results for the GPS China survey.

September 2-8	PACOM Commander, Admiral Joseph Prueher, visited China, hosted by a PLA Deputy Chief of General Staff, LTG Xiong Guangkai.
September 10	The Office for Defense Procurement/Foreign Contracting of the Under Secretary of Defense for Acquisition and Technology hosted Vice Chairman of the State Planning Commission She Jianming at the Pentagon and provided a briefing on the Defense Department's procurement system.
September 16-18	NIMA participated in the 9th meeting of the U.S.-PRC Joint Working Group for Scientific and Technical Cooperation in Surveying in Beijing.
September 17-29	A Deputy Director of the GLD, LTG Zhou Youliang, visited the United States to advance bilateral military medical relations, as the reciprocal visit for that of the Assistant Secretary of Defense for Health Affairs to China in March 1996. Both sides discussed cooperation between military hospitals, such as PLA 301 Hospital and Walter Reed Army Medical Center.
September 17	At the Pentagon, Deputy Assistant Secretary of Defense for Asian and Pacific Affairs Kurt Campbell met with the vice president of the Chinese Institute for Contemporary International Relations (CICIR), which is associated with the Ministry of State Security.
September 21-27	A team from NIMA visited China to perform maintenance on the GPS tracking station and discuss cooperative plans on gravity data.
October 4-17	Lieutenant General Xing Shizhong, President of the PLA's NDU, visited the United States. He and Lieutenant General Ervin Rokke, President of the U.S. NDU, signed a "Memorandum on Cooperation and Reciprocal Relations" between the two NDUs. They agreed to undertake reciprocal interaction on a broad range of issues relevant to professional military education, including military art, the evolution of strategy and doctrine, strategic assessment, the impact of technological advance on the nature of warfare, library science, and publishing.
October 11-17	Surgeon General of the U.S. Air Force Lieutenant General Edgar Anderson led a military medical delegation to participate in the XXXI International Congress on Military Medicine in Beijing.
October 20	At the Pentagon, Deputy Assistant Secretary of Defense for Asian and Pacific Affairs Kurt Campbell met with a delegation from the Chinese Institute of International Strategic Studies (CIISS), which is associated with the PLA.
November 11-19	The Director of DIA, Lieutenant General Patrick Hughes, visited China.
December 5-18	General Chi Haotian, a Vice Chairman of the CMC and Minister of Defense, visited the United States, to reciprocate for Defense Secretary Perry's visit to China in October 1994. Perry announced that General Chi's visit allowed for discussions of global and regional security issues as well as the future of mil-to-mil ties. While in Washington, General Chi met with President Clinton for 20 minutes. A controversy arose when General Chi gave a speech at NDU at Fort McNair and defended the PLA's crackdown on peaceful demonstrators in Beijing in 1989 (during which he was the PLA's Chief of General Staff) and claimed—apparently in a narrow sense—that no one died in Tiananmen Square itself. DOD provided a draft proposal for a bilateral military maritime cooperative agreement. The two sides agreed to continue U.S. port calls to Hong Kong after its hand-over from British to PRC control on July 1, 1997; to allow PLA ship visits to Hawaii and the U.S. west coast; to institutionalize Defense Consultative Talks; to hold senior-level visits; and to allow U.S. repatriation of the remains of the crew of a B-24 bomber that crashed in southern China in World War II (after General Chi presented dog tags found at the crash site). After Washington, Perry arranged for General Chi to travel to Air Force and Navy facilities in Norfolk, Virginia; the Air University at Maxwell Air Force Base in Alabama; Army units at Fort Hood, Texas; the Cooperative Monitoring Center at the Sandia National Laboratory in New Mexico (for discussion of technology that could be used to verify the Comprehensive Test Ban Treaty); and PACOM in Hawaii headed by Admiral Joseph Prueher.

1997

January 13-17	A Defense POW/MIA team went to Maoer Mountain in southern Guangxi province to recover the remains of a "Flying Tigers" crew whose B-24 bomber crashed into the mountain in 1944 after bombing Japanese forces near Taiwan during World War II.
January 15	At the Pentagon, Assistant Secretary of Defense for International Security Affairs Frank Kramer met with Wang Daohan, head of the Association for Relations Across the Taiwan Strait (ARATS).

February 21-March 6	LTG Kui Fulin, a Deputy Chief of General Staff, visited the United States, hosted by the Chief of Staff of the Army (CSA), General Dennis Reimer. Kui visited the Pentagon, West Point in New York, U.S. Army Forces Command in Georgia, Fort Benning in Georgia, and PACOM in Hawaii.
February 24-27	The Principal Assistant Deputy Under Secretary of Defense for Environmental Security, Gary Vest, visited Beijing to participate in the 1997 China Environment Forum and met with PLA leaders to discuss environmental security issues.
March 9-25	PLA Naval ships (the Luhu-class destroyer Harbin, the Luda-class destroyer Zhuhai, and the oiler Nanchang) visited Pearl Harbor, HI (March 9-13) and San Diego, CA (March 21-25), in the PLA Navy (PLAN)'s second ship visit to Pearl Harbor and first port call to the U.S. west coast. As part of the occasion, Vice Admiral He Pengfei (a PLAN Deputy Commander) and Vice Admiral Wang Yongguo (PLAN South Sea Fleet Commander) visited the United States.
April	Major General John Cowlings, Commandant of the Industrial College of the Armed Forces of the U.S. NDU, visited China.
May 12-15	The Chairman of the Joint Chiefs of Staff, General John Shalikashvili, visited China, hosted by the PLA's Chief of General Staff, General Fu Quanyou. On May 14, 1997, Shalikashvili gave a speech at the PLA's NDU, in which he called for mil-to-mil contacts that are deeper, more frequent, more balanced, and more developed, in order to decrease suspicion, advance cooperation, and prevent miscalculations in a crisis. He called for a more equal exchange of information, confidence building measures (CBMs), military academic and functional exchanges, the PLA's participation in multinational activities, and a regular dialogue between senior military leaders. He also urged the completion of the military maritime and air cooperative agreement. However, Shalikashvili got only a limited view of the PLA during a visit to the 15th Airborne Army (in Hubei province).
July	Lieutenant General Xu Qiliang, Chief of Staff of the PLA Air Force, led an education and training delegation to the United States.
July	LTG Wu Quanxu, a Deputy Chief of General Staff of the PLA, visited PACOM.
August 5-13	General Fu Quanyou, PLA Chief of General Staff, visited the United States. Secretary of Defense William Cohen and General John Shalikashvili welcomed Fu at the Pentagon with a 19-gun salute. General Fu also visited West Point in New York, Fort Bragg in North Carolina, Norfolk Naval Base in Virginia, Langley Air Force Base in Virginia, and PACOM in Hawaii. General Fu boarded a U.S. nuclear attack submarine and the USS *Blue Ridge*, the 7th Fleet's amphibious command ship.
September 11-15	An Arleigh Burke-class destroyer, the USS *John S. McCain*, visited Qingdao. Commander of the U.S. Pacific Fleet, Admiral Archie Clemins, visited China and met with the Commander of the PLAN North Sea Fleet, Rear Admiral Zhang Dingfa.
September 14-21	The Judge Advocate General of the U.S. Army, Major General Walter Huffman, visited China, including the Jinan MR, to discuss military law.
September 22-26	The CSA, General Dennis Reimer, visited China, along with the Army's Deputy Chief of Staff for Intelligence, LTG Claudia Kennedy. They met with Generals Chi Haotian and Fu Quanyou, and visited the 6th Tank Division and an engineering regiment in the Beijing MR, and an artillery unit in the Nanjing MR. They paid the first U.S. visit to the headquarters of the Guangzhou MR.
October 6	The Chief of Naval Operations (CNO), Admiral Jay Johnson, visited China and met with General Chi Haotian, General Fu Quanyou, and Admiral Shi Yunsheng, PLAN Commander.
October	LTG He Daoquan, a Vice President of the PLA's NDU, led a delegation to the United States (like the U.S. Capstone program for new general/flag officers).
October 29	Jiang Zemin, General Secretary of the Communist Party of China, CMC Chairman, and PRC President, visited Washington for a summit with President Clinton. Among a number of agreements, they agreed to strengthen mil-to-mil contacts to minimize miscalculations, advance transparency, and strengthen communication. In the "U.S.-PRC Joint Statement," the Administration reiterated that it adheres to the "one China" policy and the principles in the three U.S.-PRC Joint Communiques, but did not mention the Taiwan Relations Act (TRA), the law governing U.S. relations with Taiwan (including security assistance for its self-defense).
November	Continuing a POW/MIA mission, a team from the U.S. Army's Central Identification Laboratory Hawaii (CILHI) returned to Maoer Mountain in southern China to recover additional remains

	from a B-24 bomber that crashed in 1944.
December 8-19	PACOM Commander, Admiral Joseph Prueher, visited China and met with PRC leader Jiang Zemin, General Zhang Wannian, General Chi Haotian, General Fu Quanyou, among others. Prueher enjoyed what the PLA considered the broadest access ever granted to a visiting military official during one trip. Prueher visited the Jinan, Nanjing, and Guangzhou MRs. He visited the PLAAF Flight Test and Development Center in Cangzhou in Jinan, where he saw a static display of aircraft, after poor weather apparently precluded a flight demonstration of F-7 and F-8 fighters. Prueher visited the 179th Infantry Division at the Nanjing MR, watched a live-fire assault demonstration, and toured a farm run by the PLA. At Zhanjiang, Prueher visited the PLA Navy's South Sea Fleet, where he observed a demonstration by the 1st Marine Brigade, saw a new air-cushioned landing craft, and toured the destroyer Zhuhai. Prueher stressed future PLA-PACOM cooperation in peacekeeping and disaster relief training.
December 11-12	LTG Xiong Guangkai, a PLA Deputy Chief of General Staff, visited the Pentagon to hold the 1st U.S.-PLA Defense Consultative Talks (DCT) with Under Secretary of Defense for Policy Walter Slocombe. During their summit in October, Presidents Clinton and Jiang had agreed to hold regular rounds of DCT. The two sides initialed the Military Maritime Consultative Agreement (MMCA) ("Agreement Between the Department of Defense of the United States of America and the Ministry of National Defense of the People's Republic of China on Establishing a Consultation Mechanism to Strengthen Military Maritime Safety").
December	The U.S. Air Force and Coast Guard conducted search-and-rescue exercises in Hong Kong (with its Civil Aviation Department), after the British hand-over of Hong Kong to PRC sovereignty in July 1997. At a briefing on July 7, 1998, the Pentagon said that the PLA observed this exercise.
December	A PLA training delegation visited the U.S. Army's premier National Training Center (NTC) at Fort Irwin in California.

1998

January 17-21	Secretary of Defense William Cohen, accompanied by Admiral Prueher (PACOM Commander), visited China. Cohen signed the "Military Maritime Consultative Agreement (MMCA)," intended to set up a framework for dialogue on how to minimize the chances of miscalculation and accidents between U.S. and PLA forces operating at sea or in the air. He said that Jiang Zemin and General Chi Haotian promised that China did not plan to transfer to Iran additional anti-ship cruise missiles. The PLA allowed Cohen to be the first Western official to visit the Beijing MR's Air Defense Command Center, a step that Cohen called important and symbolic. However, the PLA denied Cohen's request to visit China's National Command Center. Cohen gave a speech at the PLA's AMS and called for expanded mil-to-mil contacts on: (1) defense environmental issues; (2) strategic nuclear missile forces; (3) POW/MIA affairs; and (4) humanitarian operations (as part of shifting contacts from those that build confidence to those that advance real-world cooperation). Cohen asked the PLA to allow U.S. access to PRC archives for answers about the fate of U.S. POW/MIAs in the Korean War who might have been in prison camps in China.
February 16-20	For the first time, the PLA attended the Pacific Area Special Operations Conference (PASOC) in Hawaii.
March 14-24	A U.S. Army training delegation from the Training and Doctrine Command (TRADOC) based at Fort Monroe, VA, visited China. The Deputy Chief of Staff for Training, Major General Leroy Goff and Assistant Deputy Chief of Staff for Personnel, Major General David Ohle, led the delegation. They saw the PLA's training base in Anhui province under the Nanjing MR (similar to the NTC), then curtailed the visit to go to Hong Kong due to the PLA's insufficient reciprocity.
March 29-April 10	General Wang Ke, Director of the GLD of the PLA, visited the United States, hosted by the Under Secretary of Defense for Acquisitions and Technology. General Wang visited West Point in New York, Aberdeen Proving Ground in Maryland, the Pentagon, Warner-Robins Air Logistics Center in Georgia, the Defense Logistics Agency's Defense Supply Center in Richmond, the USS Abraham Lincoln aircraft carrier at Naval Air Station North Island (San Diego) in California, and PACOM in Hawaii. At the Pentagon, DOD provided briefings on: organizations for the DOD Logistics Systems, Logistics Modernization Initiatives, Joint Logistics/Focused Logistics, DOD Outsourcing Process and Experiences, DOD Military Retirement Systems, and the Army's Integrated Training Area Management Program.

In April 1998, the *New York Times* disclosed that the Justice Department began a criminal investigation into whether U.S. satellite manufacturers, Loral Space and Communications Ltd. and Hughes Electronics Corporation, violated export control laws. They allegedly provided expertise that China could use to improve its ballistic missiles, when the companies shared their technical findings with China on the cause of its rocket's explosion while launching a U.S.-origin satellite in February 1996. The House set up the "Cox Committee" to investigate the allegations of corporate misconduct and policy mistakes. The Senate set up a task force. Congress passed legislation to control satellite exports to China. The Cox Committee, formally called the House Select Committee on U.S. National Security and Military/Commercial Concerns with the People's Republic of China, issued its unclassified report in May 1999.

April 6-10	The PLA went to PACOM's Military Operations and Law Conference, organized by the Judge Advocate's office.
April 29-30	The Defense Department and PLA held pre-talks on the Military Maritime Consultative Agreement (MMCA).
May 3-5	Assistant Secretary of Defense for International Security Affairs Franklin Kramer visited Beijing.
May 4-9	The Chief of Staff of the Air Force (CSAF), General Michael Ryan, visited China. The PLAAF gave him a tour of Foshan Air Base and allowed him to fly an F-7 fighter and view an air-refuelable version of an FA-2. However, the PLAAF denied Ryan's requests to fly in a SU-27 fighter, to see integration of the SU-27s into the units, and to learn about development of the F-10 fighter.
May	A PLA delegation on military law visited the United States.
June 25-July 3	President Clinton traveled to China to hold his 2nd summit with Jiang Zemin, following the summit in October 1997. They announced that the United States and China: have a direct presidential "hot line" that was set up in May 1998; will not target strategic nuclear weapons under their respective control at each other; will hold the first meeting under the MMCA; will observe exercises of the other based on reciprocity (meaning the PLA would also issue invitations to U.S. observers); will cooperate in humanitarian assistance; and will cooperate in military environmental security. However, China only agreed to study whether to join the Missile Technology Control Regime (MTCR) and did not agree to open archives to allow U.S. research on POW/MIAs from the Korean War. In Shanghai on June 30, Clinton stated the so-called "Three Noes" of non-support for Taiwan's independence; non-support for two Chinas or one China and one Taiwan; and non-support for Taiwan's membership in international bodies requiring statehood.
July 9-24	At U.S. invitation, the PLA sent two observers to Cope Thunder 98-4, a multinational air exercise held at Eielson and Elmendorf Air Force Bases in Alaska. The air forces of the United States, United Kingdom, Australia, Japan, and Singapore participated in the exercise, which was designed to sharpen air combat skills, exchange air operational tactics, and promote closer relations. Pilots flew a variety of aircraft in air-to-air and air-to-ground combat missions, and combat support missions against a realistic set of threats. Russia, Brunei, Malaysia, Thailand, and the Philippines sent military observers.
July 14-15	In Beijing, the DOD and PLA held the first plenary meeting under the MMCA.
July 15-20	At U.S. invitation, the PLA Navy sent two observers to RIMPAC 1998, the first time the PLA observed this multinational naval exercise based in Hawaii in the Pacific Ocean. The naval forces of the United States, Australia, Canada, Chile, Japan, and South Korea participated in the exercise, which was designed to enhance their tactical capabilities in maritime operations. During part of the exercise, the U.S. Navy hosted the PLA Navy's representatives on board the USS *Coronado* (the 3rd Fleet's command ship), the USS *Carl Vinson* aircraft carrier, the USS *Paul Hamilton* (an Arleigh Burke-class destroyer), and the USS *Antietam* (a Ticonderoga-class cruiser).
July 20-26	PLA Deputy Chief of General Staff, LTG Qian Shugen, visited the United States.
July	A PRC civilian and military delegation visited the United States, including Pensacola, FL, to discuss air traffic control with the Federal Aviation Administration, Departments of Commerce and Defense, and the U.S. Air Force.

August 2-6	The command ship of the 7th Fleet, USS *Blue Ridge*, and a destroyer, USS *John S. McCain*, visited Qingdao. As part of the occasion, Vice Admiral Robert Natter, Commander of the 7th Fleet, visited and met with Vice Admiral Shi Yunsheng, PLAN Commander, and Vice Admiral He Pengfei, a PLAN Deputy Commander.
August 16-23	The Commandant of the Army War College, Major General Robert Scales, and the U.S. Army's Chief of Military History, Brigadier General John Mountcastle, visited Beijing, Tianjin, and Nanjing, and discussed the PLA's historical campaigns.
September 12-20	NDU President, LTG Richard Chilcoat, visited Hong Kong, Beijing, Xian, and Dalian.
September 14-24	General Zhang Wannian, a Politburo Member, a Vice Chairman of the CMC, and highest ranking PLA officer, visited the United States. However, with General Shalikashvili's disappointment with the lack of transparency and reciprocity shown to him by the PLA during his trip to China in May 1997, Secretary of Defense William Cohen invoked the "Shali Prohibitions" in restricting General Zhang's exposure to the U.S. military during his visits to the Pentagon, Fort Benning in Georgia, and Nellis Air Force Base in Nevada. President Clinton met briefly with General Zhang at the White House during his meeting with National Security Advisor Samuel Berger. At a news conference on September 15, 1998, Secretary Cohen announced that he and General Zhang signed an agreement on cooperation in environmental security ("Joint Statement on the Exchange of Information by the United States Department of Defense and the Chinese Ministry of National Defense on Military Environmental Protection"); discussed weapons proliferation and international terrorism; and agreed to conduct sand table exercises on disaster relief and humanitarian assistance in 1999, to have a ship visit by the PLA Navy in 1999, to conduct a seminar on maritime search and rescue, to allow each other to observe specific military exercises, to exchange military students, and to allow a PRC delegation to visit the Cooperative Monitoring Center at the Sandia National Laboratory. However, Cohen did not announce any progress in following up on U.S. concerns about Korean War POW/MIA cases, non-targeting of strategic nuclear forces (involving the Strategic Command (STRATCOM) and the PLA's Second Artillery), PLA threats against Taiwan, or weapons nonproliferation. General Zhang cited President Clinton's statements in China in June about the U.S. "one China" policy and the "Three Noes," while Secretary Cohen stressed peaceful resolution and said that Clinton reiterated commitment to the Taiwan Relations Act.
October 20-21	Under Secretary of Defense for Policy Walter Slocombe visited Beijing for the 2nd DCT and met with Generals Zhang Wannian and Chi Haotian (CMC Vice Chairmen), and LTG Xiong Guangkai. They discussed global and regional concerns, defense relations in Asia-Pacific, military strategy and modernization, and mil-to-mil contacts in 1999 ("Gameplan for 1999 U.S.-Sino Defense Exchanges"). The PLA raised objections to the U.S. plan to field theater missile defense systems.
November 1	Secretary of Defense Cohen visited Hong Kong (on his way to South Korea and Japan) to underscore the U.S. determination to continue its defense involvement there, including ship visits, after its hand-over to PRC rule.
November 9-14	PACOM Commander, Admiral Joseph Prueher, visited China, along with LTG Carl Fulford (Commander of U.S. Marine Forces Pacific) and Major General Earl Hailston (Director for Strategic Planning and Policy). They met with General Zhang Wannian (a CMC Vice Chairman), General Fu Quanyou (Chief of General Staff), General Wang Ke (GLD Director), and LTG Xiong Guangkai (a Deputy Chief of General Staff). The PLA arranged for visits to the 47th Group Army based near Xian and a subordinate air defense brigade, in granting the first foreign military access to these two commands. Prueher also visited the PLAAF's 28th Air Attack Division in Hangzhou and observed ordnance loading of A-5 bombers and a live-fire demonstration of an air-to-ground attack by A-5s. He then toured a Jiangwei-class frigate of the PLAN in Shanghai.
December 1-4	U.S. and PLA military forces participated in an annual search and rescue exercise (HK SAREX 98) held by Hong Kong's Civil Aviation Department.
December 4	PACOM Commander, Admiral Joseph Prueher, visited Hong Kong and met with Major Generals Zhou Borong and Xiong Ziren, Deputy Commander and Political Commissar of PLA forces there.

December 4-8	A U.S. Navy frigate, the USS *Vandegrift*, visited Shanghai. As part of the port call, Rear Admiral Harry Highfill, Commander of the U.S. 7th Fleet's Amphibious Force, met with Rear Admiral Hou Yuexi, Commander of the Shanghai Naval Base. The PLAN arranged for Admiral Highfill to tour the PLAN's Jiangwei-class frigate, the Anqing.
December 9-11	Military maritime consultative talks (under the MMCA) between the U.S. Navy and PLAN took place near San Diego, CA. The PLAN delegation, led by Captain Shen Hao, Director of the PLAN Operations Department, stayed at the Naval Amphibious Base at Coronado and toured a U.S. destroyer (USS *Stetham*) and the U.S. Navy's Maritime Ship Handling Simulator at the San Diego Naval Station.

1999

At the end of 1998 and start of 1999, the *New York Times* and *Wall Street Journal* disclosed that the Cox Committee was looking at the Clinton Administration's investigation that began in 1995 into whether China obtained secret U.S. nuclear weapons data, in addition to missile technology associated with satellite launches. On April 21, 1999, the Director of Central Intelligence confirmed that "China obtained by espionage classified U.S. nuclear weapons information that probably accelerated its program to develop future nuclear weapons." However, it was uncertain whether China obtained documentation or blueprints, and China also benefitted from information obtained from a wide variety of sources, including open sources (unclassified information) and China's own efforts.

January 19-26	The Director of the Defense POW/MIA Office, Deputy Assistant Secretary of Defense Robert Jones, visited China to seek the PLA's cooperation in accounting for U.S. POW/MIAs from the Korean War, specifically seeking U.S. access to PLA archives, veterans, and a film with information about POW camps in China.
March	President of the PLA's NDU, General Xing Shizhong, visited Washington and gave a speech at the U.S. NDU at Fort McNair on March 18, 1999. The Pentagon arranged for General Xing to visit Norfolk Naval Base in Virginia, receive a briefing on the U.S. Navy's "Network Centric Warfare" in Rhode Island, visit Fort Hood in Texas and receive a briefing on Task Force XXI (an experimental warfighting force in the Army), and see the Air Warfare Center at Nellis Air Force Base in Nevada. However, the Defense Department denied the PLA delegation's access to observe the Red Flag combat training exercise at Nellis Air Force Base.

On May 7, 1999, U.S.-led NATO forces bombed the PRC's embassy in Belgrade, Yugoslavia, having mistakenly targeted it as a military supply facility belonging to Yugoslav President Slobodan Milosevic, whose Serbian forces attacked Kosovo. Despite President Clinton's apology, the PRC angrily suspended mil-to-mil contacts, allowed protesters to violently attack U.S. diplomatic facilities in China, and denied ship visits to Hong Kong by the U.S. Navy until September 1999. On May 8, Secretary of State Madeleine Albright wrote a letter to the PRC Foreign Minister to express "sincere sorrow" for loss of life, injuries, and damage as a result of the mistaken bombing with no intention to hit the PRC embassy. She also expressed critical concern about China allowing large-scale demonstrations at the U.S. Embassy and Consulates that were "threatening the safety of our officials and their families and causing damage to our properties." The Ambassador was trapped at the U.S. Embassy. PRC protestors burned a building at the Consulate in Chengdu. Then-PRC Vice President Hu Jintao expressed support for what he called "legal protests." Testifying to Congress, Defense Secretary William Cohen warned China against "exacerbating" tension and "calculated exploitation." In July 1999, the United States agreed to pay $4.5 million in compensation for PRC casualties. In FY2001 legislation, Congress appropriated $28 million to compensate for damages to China's embassy.

May	A U.S. Navy working group under the MMCA visited Qingdao to discuss international standards of communication at sea.
May 9-20	A PRC delegation that included PLA officers visited the United States to discuss air traffic control. On May 18, 1999, they visited Edwards Air Force Base in California and received a briefing on daily planning, integration, and control of civilian and military operations.

> On July 9, 1999, Taiwan President Lee Teng-hui characterized the cross-strait relationship as "special state-to-state ties," sparking military tensions with the PLA. The Clinton Administration responded that Lee's statement was not helpful and reaffirmed the "one China" policy. The PLA flew fighters across the "center" line of the Taiwan Strait and conducted exercises along the coast opposite Taiwan. In early September, CMC Vice Chairman General Zhang Wannian personally directed a joint landing exercise. An earthquake in Taiwan on September 21 defused the tension.

November 19-21	Deputy Assistant Secretary of Defense for Asian and Pacific Affairs Kurt Campbell and Major General (USMC) Michael Hagee, PACOM's Director for Strategic Planning and Policy (J5), visited Beijing to discuss resuming military contacts.
December 1-4	U.S. military and PLA participated in Hong Kong's annual search and rescue exercise.

2000

January 24-26	Resuming contacts, LTG Xiong Guangkai (a Deputy Chief of General Staff) visited Washington to hold the 3rd DCT with Under Secretary of Defense for Policy Slocombe. They discussed the program for mil-to-mil contacts in 2000, international security issues, U.S. strategy in Asia, the PLA's missile buildup, Taiwan, missile defense, weapons proliferation, and North Korea. Xiong met with Secretary of Defense Cohen, Chairman of the Joint Chiefs General Henry Shelton, Deputy National Security Advisor James Steinberg, Under Secretary of State Thomas Pickering, and State Department Senior Advisor John Holum.
February 17-18	Deputy Secretary of State Strobe Talbott, Under Secretary of Defense for Policy Walter Slocombe, Vice Chairman of the Joint Chiefs of Staff General Joseph Ralston, and Deputy National Security Advisor James Steinberg visited Beijing (after visiting Tokyo) for a strategic dialogue. They met with CMC Vice Chairman General Zhang Wannian, who raised concerns about Taiwan, including U.S. arms sales to Taiwan.

> On February 21, 2000, ahead of Taiwan's presidential election on March 18, 2000, the PRC issued its second Taiwan White Paper, which declared a threat to use force against Taiwan if a serious development leads to Taiwan's separation from China in any name, if there is foreign invasion or occupation of Taiwan, or if Taiwan's government indefinitely refuses to negotiate national unification (called the "Three Ifs"). Under Secretary of Defense Slocombe, who was just in Beijing but was given no indication that the PRC would issue the White Paper and the threat, responded forcefully on February 22 by warning that China would face "incalculable consequences" if it used force against Taiwan.

February 27-March 2	PACOM Commander, Admiral Dennis Blair, visited China and discussed tensions over Taiwan with Chief of General Staff, General Fu Quanyou, and General Chi Haotian.
March 10-12	Secretary of Defense William Cohen visited Hong Kong and discussed issues such as port calls by the U.S. Navy and the prevention of trans-shipments of advanced U.S. technology to mainland China.
March 27-29	A working group under the MMCA held a planning meeting in China.
April 14-22	PLAN Commander, Admiral Shi Yunsheng, visited the United States, coinciding with an annual round of U.S.-Taiwan arms sales talks in Washington. Admiral Shi met with Secretary of Defense Cohen, Vice Chairman of the Joint Chiefs of Staff General Richard Myers, and Chief of Naval Operations Admiral Jay Johnson.
May 28-June 3	PACOM in Hawaii hosted the second plenary meeting under the MMCA. PACOM's Director for Strategic Planning and Policy (J5), Major General Michael Hagee (USMC), and the PLA's Deputy Chief of Staff, Rear Admiral Wang Yucheng, led the proceedings. They reviewed a mutually-produced document, "A Study on Sino-U.S. Maritime Navigational Safety, Including Communications."
June 13-14	Assistant Secretary of Defense for International Security Affairs Frank Kramer visited Beijing and met with Major General Zhan Maohai, LTG Xiong Guangkai, and General Chi Haotian to plan Secretary of Defense Cohen's visit to China.

June 13-21	Superintendent of the U.S. Military Academy (West Point), LTG Daniel Christman, visited China. He met with General Chi Haotian and visited the PLA's Armored Force Engineering Academy, where he was the first American to have access to a PLA Type-96 main battle tank.
June 18-23	Nanjing MR Commander Liang Guanglie led a PLA delegation to visit PACOM in Hawaii and met with Admiral Dennis Blair.

On July 10, 2000, responding to objections from the Clinton Administration and Congress, Israeli Prime Minister Ehud Barak told PRC ruler Jiang Zemin in a letter that Israel canceled the nearly completed sale of the Phalcon airborne early warning system to the PLA. Prime Minister Barak informed President Clinton the next day during peace talks at Camp David, MD.

July 11-15	Secretary of Defense William Cohen visited Beijing and Shanghai. Cohen met with President Jiang Zemin and Generals Chi Haotian, Zhang Wannian, and Fu Quanyou. Cohen did not visit any PLA bases. Cohen referred to the promise made by PRC President Jiang Zemin during Cohen's previous visit to China in January 1998 and said that the PRC has abided by that agreement not to ship cruise missiles to Iran. Cohen and General Chi signed an "Agreement on the Exchange of Environmental Protection Research and Development Information" and discussed the need for cross-strait dialogue, weapons nonproliferation, and regional stability. The PRC objected to U.S. plans for missile defense and pressure on Israel to cancel the sale of the Phalcon airborne early warning system to the PLA, concerning which Israel notified China just before Cohen's visit. Cohen offered to fund PLA students at PACOM's APCSS in Honolulu. Regarding Taiwan, General Chi said that China would adopt a wait and see posture toward the leader of Taiwan (referring to Chen Shui-bian of the Democratic Progressive Party, who won the presidential election on March 18, 2000, bringing an end to the Kuomintang (KMT)'s 55 years of rule in Taiwan). Cohen said that the Administration viewed Chen as offering hope for cross-strait reconciliation. In Shanghai, Cohen stepped out of the narrow mil-to-mil context and met with Wang Daohan, chairman of the PRC's Association for Relations Across the Taiwan Strait (ARATS). Cohen said that Chen showed flexibility after becoming president and that there was a window of opportunity for changes.
July 23-August 4	A delegation of the PLA Medical Department visited the United States.
July 31-August 5	Admiral Thomas Fargo, Commander of the U.S. Pacific Fleet, visited Beijing and Qingdao in conjunction with the visit of the U.S. Navy's guided-missile cruiser USS *Chancellorsville* in Qingdao (August 2-5).
August 21- September 2	President of the PLA's AMS, General Wang Zuxun, visited the United States. There is no counterpart in the U.S. military with which to set up reciprocal exchanges. The AMS delegation included the Directors of the Departments of Strategic Studies, Operational and Tactical Studies, and Foreign Military Studies. They visited the Pentagon; Joint Forces Command in Norfolk, Virginia; West Point in New York; Army War College in Pennsylvania; Army's Training and Doctrine Command (TRADOC) at Fort Monroe in Virginia; and PACOM in Hawaii. The Joint Forces Command provided unclassified tours of its Joint Training Directorate (J-7) and Joint Training Analysis Simulation Center, but not the Joint Experimentation Battle Lab.
September 5-18	PLA Navy ships (the Luhu-class destroyer Qingdao and Fuqing-class oiler Taicang) visited Pearl Harbor, HI (September 5-8) and Naval Station Everett, near Seattle, WA (September 14-18). In Hawaii, the visitors toured the U.S. destroyer USS *O'Kane*.
October	For the first time, the PLA invited two U.S. military personnel to attend the one-month International Security Symposium at the NDU in Beijing. (Subsequent invitations dropped required fees.)
October 10-18	The PLA participated in a visit to the United States by a Humanitarian Disaster Relief Sandtable Planning Team.
October 12-13	Secretary of the Navy Richard Danzig visited Shanghai, in the first visit by a U.S. Secretary of the Navy to China. His visit was curtailed because of the attack on the USS *Cole* in a Yemeni harbor on October 12, 2000.

October 24- November 4	CMC Member and Director of the General Political Department (GPD)—the top political commissar, General Yu Yongbo, visited the United States. He was hosted by Under Secretary of Defense for Readiness Bernard Rostker. General Yu's delegation visited the Pentagon and met with Secretary of Defense Cohen; West Point in NY; Bolling Air Force Base in Washington, DC; Fort Jackson in SC; Patrick Air Force Base in FL; and PACOM in HI.
November 2-6	Chairman of the Joint Chiefs of Staff, General Henry Shelton, visited China, at the invitation of Chief of General Staff, General Fu Quanyou. The PLA allowed Shelton to observe a brigade exercising at the Combined Arms Training Center in the Nanjing MR. Shelton stressed the peaceful resolution of the Taiwan question.
November 2-12	A Deputy Chief of Staff of the PLA Navy, Rear Admiral Zhang Zhannan, led a delegation from the Naval Command Academy (in Nanjing) to visit Newport News, RI (Naval War College); Washington, DC (including a meeting with the Secretary of the Navy); Monterey, CA (Naval Post-Graduate School); and Honolulu, HI (PACOM, including a tour aboard an Aegis-equipped cruiser).
November 12-19	A PLA NDU delegation (similar to the U.S. Capstone program) visited the United States.
November 28- December 2	Under Secretary of Defense for Policy Walter Slocombe visited Beijing to hold the 4th DCT with PLA Deputy Chief of General Staff Xiong Guangkai. Slocombe also met with Generals Chi Haotian and Fu Quanyou and visited the PLA Navy's North Sea Fleet in Qingdao. The U.S. and PRC sides discussed sharp differences over Taiwan and missile defense, the program for mil-to-mil contacts in 2001, Korea, and weapons proliferation.
December 3-9	A Working Group under the MMCA held its second meeting (in China).
December 5-8	U.S. military and PLA forces participated in Hong Kong's annual search and rescue exercise and worked together in a demonstration.

At the end of December 2000 in New York, PLA Senior Colonel Xu Junping, who closely handled U.S.-PRC military relations, defected to the United States and presented an intelligence loss for the PLA (reported *Far Eastern Economic Review*, April 5, 2001).

2001

February 9-23	Major General Wang Shouye, Director of the GLD's Capital Construction and Barracks Department, led a delegation on military environmental protection matters to the United States. They visited Washington, DC; Fort Pickett in Virginia; Fort Bliss in Texas; the "boneyard" at Davis-Monthan Air Force Base in Arizona; Las Vegas in Nevada; and PACOM in Hawaii.
March 14-17	PACOM Commander, Adm. Dennis Blair, visited Beijing, Nanjing, and Shanghai. PACOM said that Blair's trip was intended to discuss military activities and plans of the PLA and PACOM, exchange views and enhance mutual understanding, discuss Taiwan, and stress the inclusion rather than exclusion of China in multilateral activities.
March 23-26	The command ship of the 7th Fleet, the USS *Blue Ridge*, made a port call to Shanghai. In conjunction with the ship visit, Vice Admiral James Metzger, Commander of the 7th Fleet, visited Shanghai and met with Vice Admiral Zhao Guojun, Commander of the PLAN's East Sea Fleet.

On March 24, 2001, in the Yellow Sea near South Korea, a PLA Navy Jianghu III-class frigate passed as close as 100 yards to a U.S. surveillance ship, the USNS *Bowditch*, and a PLA reconnaissance plane shadowed it. The PLA's harassment of the USS *Bowditch* continued for months.

On April 1, 2001, a PLA Navy F-8 fighter collided with a U.S. Navy EP-3 reconnaissance plane over the South China Sea. Upon surviving the collision, the EP-3's crew made an emergency landing on China's Hainan island. The PLA detained the 24 U.S. Navy personnel for 11 days. Instead of acknowledging that the PLA had started aggressive interceptions of U.S. reconnaissance flights in December 2000 and apologizing for the accident, top PRC ruler Jiang Zemin demanded an apology and compensation from the United States. The United States did not transport the damaged EP-3 out of China until July 3.

On April 24, 2001, during the last annual arms sales talks in Washington, President Bush approved requests from Taiwan's military to purchase weapons systems including diesel-electric submarines; P-3 anti-submarine warfare aircraft; and destroyers (approving four Kidd-class destroyers). The Bush Administration also decided to brief Taiwan on the PAC-3 missile defense missile. The next day, the President said in an interview that if the PRC attacked Taiwan, the United States would have an obligation to do "whatever it took to help Taiwan defend herself."

September 14-15	DOD and the PLA held a special meeting under the MMCA (in Guam) to discuss how to avoid clashes like the one involving the EP-3. The Commander of U.S. Naval Forces Marianas, Rear Admiral Tom Fellin, led the U.S. delegation. The issues for U.S. side were: principles of safe flight and navigation for military activities conducted on the high seas, international airspace, and EEZs; and safety of ships and aircraft exercising the right of distressed entry. The Deputy Director of the Foreign Affairs Office, Major General Zhang Bangdong, led the PLA delegation.
December 5-7	A Working Group under the MMCA met in Beijing.

2002

April 10-12	The third plenary meeting under the MMCA was held in Shanghai. PACOM's Director for Strategic Planning and Policy (J5), Rear Admiral William Sullivan, and the PLA Navy's Deputy Chief of Staff, Rear Admiral Zhou Borong, led the delegations.
April 27-May 1	PRC Vice President Hu Jintao visited PACOM and was welcomed by Admiral Dennis Blair. In Washington, Secretary of Defense Rumsfeld welcomed Hu with an honor cordon at the Pentagon. PRC media reported that Rumsfeld and Hu reached a consensus to resume military exchanges, but the Pentagon's spokeswoman said that they agreed to have their representatives talk about how to proceed on mil-to-mil contacts, which were still approved on a case-by-case basis. Vice President Hu also met with President Bush and Vice President Dick Cheney.
May 14-28	For the first time, the PLA sent observers to Cobra Gold 2002 in Thailand, a combined exercise involving forces of the United States, Thailand, and Singapore. Senators Jesse Helms and Robert Smith expressed their concerns to the Secretary of Defense.
June 26-27	Assistant Secretary of Defense for International Security Affairs Peter Rodman visited Beijing to discuss a resumption of military exchanges. He met with General Xiong Guangkai and General Chi Haotian, who said that the PRC was ready to improve military relations with the United States. Secretary Rumsfeld told reporters on June 21, 2002, that Rodman would discuss the principles of transparency, reciprocity, and consistency for mil-to-mil contacts that Rumsfeld stressed to Vice President Hu Jintao.
July 15-29	In the first POW/MIA mission in China on a Cold War case, a team from the Army's Central Identification Laboratory in Hawaii (CILHI) went to northeastern Jilin province to search for, but did not find, the remains of two CIA pilots whose C-47 plane was shot down in 1952 during the Korean War.
August 6-8	The PLA and DOD held a meeting under the MMCA in Hawaii.
August-September	In a POW/MIA recovery mission, a team from the Army's Central Identification Laboratory in Hawaii (CILHI) recovered remains of the crew of a C-46 cargo plane that crashed in March 1944 in Tibet while flying the "Hump" route over the Himalaya mountains back to India from Kunming, China, during World War II. The two-month operation excavated a site at 15,600 ft.

In September 2002, PLA patrol aircraft and ships harassed the unarmed USNS *Bowditch* in international water in the Yellow Sea. The PLA claimed the ship's surveys violated the PRC's EEZ. The two countries traded diplomatic protests.

October 8-14	The President of NDU, Vice Admiral Paul Gaffney, visited Beijing, Xian, Hangzhou, and Shanghai. He met with CMC Vice Chairman and Defense Minister Chi Haotian, Deputy Chief of General Staff Xiong Guangkai, and NDU President Xing Shizhong.
October 25	President Bush held a summit with PRC President Jiang Zemin at his ranch in Crawford, TX. Concerning security issues, President Bush said they discussed "the threat posed by the Iraqi regime," "concern about the acknowledgment of the Democratic People's Republic of Korea of a

program to enrich uranium," counterterrorism (calling China an "ally"), weapons proliferation, Taiwan, and a "candid, constructive, and cooperative" relationship with contacts at many levels in coming months, including "a new dialogue on security issues." Jiang offered a vague proposal to reconsider the PLA's missile buildup in return for restraints in U.S. arms sales to Taiwan.

November 24	In the first U.S. naval port call to mainland China since the EP-3 crisis, the destroyer USS *Paul F. Foster* visited Qingdao.
November 30-December 8	LTG Gao Jindian, a Vice President of the NDU, led a Capstone-like delegation to the United States.
December 4-6	The Maritime and Air Safety Working Group under the MMCA met in Qingdao. The U.S. team toured the destroyer Qingdao.
December 9-10	Following a two-year hiatus after the previous Defense Consultative Talks (DCT) in December 2000, the Pentagon held the 5th DCT (the first under the Bush Administration) and kept U.S. representation at the same level as that under the Clinton Administration. Under Secretary of Defense for Policy Douglas Feith met with General Xiong Guangkai, a Deputy Chief of General Staff, at the Pentagon. The PLA played up the status of Xiong and the DCT, calling the meeting "defense consultations at the vice ministerial level." At U.S. urging, Xiong brought a proposal for mil-to-mil exchanges in 2003. Feith told reporters that he could not claim progress in gaining greater reciprocity and transparency in the exchanges, although they had a discussion of these issues. They did not discuss Jiang's offer on the PLA's missile buildup. Feith also said that DOD had no major change in its attitude toward the PLA since the EP-3 crisis. Secretary Rumsfeld did not meet with Xiong. Deputy Secretary of Defense Wolfowitz and National Security Advisor Condoleezza Rice met with Xiong on December 10.
December 12-17	PACOM Commander, Admiral Thomas Fargo, visited Chengdu, Nanjing, Ningbo, Be jing, and Shanghai. The PLA showed him a live-fire exercise conducted by a reserve unit of an infantry division in Sichuan. General Liang Guanglie (Chief of General Staff) met with Admiral Fargo.

2003

March 25-29	The Director of the Defense POW/MIA Office (DPMO), Deputy Assistant Secretary of Defense Jerry Jennings, visited China and met with officials of the PLA, Ministry of Foreign Affairs (MFA), and Red Cross Society of China. Jennings said that the PRC has records that may well hold "the key" to helping DOD to resolve many of the cases of American POWs and MIAs from the Vietnam War, the Korean War, and the Cold War. While the PRC has been "very cooperative" in U.S. investigations of losses from World War II and Vietnam, Jennings said both sides suggested ways to "enhance cooperation" on Korean War cases and acknowledged that there is limited time. Jennings sought access to information in PRC archives at the national and provincial levels, assistance from PRC civilian researchers to conduct archival research on behalf of the United States, information from the Dandong Museum relating to two F-86 pilots who are Korean War MIAs, and resumption of contact with PLA veterans from the Korean War to build on information related to the PRC operation of POW camps during the war.
April 9-11	In Hawaii, in the fourth plenary meeting under the MMCA, PACOM's Director for Strategic Planning and Policy (J5), Rear Admiral William Sullivan, met with PLA Navy's Deputy Chief of Staff, Rear Admiral Zhou Borong.
April 25-May 4	The Commandant of the PLA's NDU, LTG Pei Huailiang, led a delegation to visit the U.S. Naval Academy in Annapolis, MD; U.S. NDU in Washington, DC; Marine Corps Recruit Depot in San Diego, CA; and PACOM in Honolulu, HI.
May 15-29	The PLA sent observers to Cobra Gold 2003 in Thailand, a combined exercise involving the armed forces of the United States, Thailand, and Singapore.
August 19-21	The Military Maritime and Air Safety Working Group under the MMCA met in Hawaii. The PLA met with PACOM's Chief of Staff for the Director for Strategic Planning and Policy, Brigadier General (USAF) Charles Neeley, and toured the U.S. Aegis-equipped cruiser USS *Lake Erie*.
August 25	The PLA arranged for 27 military observers from the United States and other countries to be the first foreign military observers to visit China's largest combined arms training base (in the Inner Mongolia Autonomous Region) and watch an exercise that involved elements of force-on-force, live-fire, and joint operational maneuvers conducted by the Beijing MR.

September 22-26   In the first foreign naval ship visit to Zhanjiang, the cruiser USS *Cowpens* and frigate USS *Vandegrift* visited this homeport of the PLAN's South Sea Fleet. Its Chief of Staff, Rear Admiral Hou Yuexi, welcomed Rear Admiral James Kelly, Commander of Carrier Group Five, who also visited.

October 22-25   The PLAN destroyer Shenzhen and supply ship Qinghai Lake visited Guam.

October 24-
November 1   Politburo Member, CMC Vice Chairman, and PRC Defense Minister, General Cao Gangchuan, visited PACOM in Hawaii, West Point in New York, and Washington, DC, where he met with Secretary of Defense Donald Rumsfeld and Secretary of State Colin Powell. General Cao stressed that Taiwan was the most important dispute. The PLA sought the same treatment for General Cao as that given to General Chi Haotian when he visited Washington as defense minister in 1996 and was granted a meeting with President Clinton. In the end, President Bush dropped by for five minutes when General Cao met with National Security Advisor Rice at the White House. Rumsfeld did not attend the PRC Embassy's banquet for Cao. At PACOM, Cao met with Admiral Thomas Fargo and toured the cruiser USS *Lake Erie*.

November 12-19   Nanjing MR Commander, LTG Zhu Wenquan, visited PACOM where he met with Admiral Thomas Fargo and boarded the destroyer USS *Russell*. Zhu visited San Diego, where he toured the carrier USS *Nimitz* and the Marine Corps Recruit Depot. He also stopped in Washington and West Point in New York.

On November 18, 2003, a PRC official on Taiwan affairs who is a PLA major general, Wang Zaixi, issued a threat to use force against the perceived open promotion of Taiwan independence. Campaigning for reelection on March 20, 2004, Taiwan's President Chen Shui-bian was calling for controversial referendums and a new Taiwan constitution. On the eve of his visit to Washington, PRC Premier Wen Jiabao threatened that China would "pay any price to safeguard the unity of the motherland." On December 3, PRC media reported the warnings of a PLA major general and a senior colonel at AMS, who wrote that Chen's use of referendums to seek independence will push Taiwan into the "abyss of war." They warned that China would be willing to pay the costs of war, including boycotts of the 2008 Olympics in Beijing, drops in foreign investment, setbacks in foreign relations, wartime damage to the southeastern coast, economic costs, and PLA casualties. Appearing with Premier Wen at the White House on December 9, 2003, President Bush criticized Chen, saying that "we oppose any unilateral decision by either China or Taiwan to change the status quo. And the comments and actions made by the leader of Taiwan indicate that he may be willing to make decisions unilaterally to change the status quo, which we oppose."

2004

January 13-16   The Chairman of the Joint Chiefs of Staff, General (USAF) Richard Myers, visited Beijing, the first visit to China by the highest ranking U.S. military officer since November 2000. General Myers met with Generals Guo Boxiong and Cao Gangchuan (CMC Vice Chairmen) and General Liang Guanglie (PLA Chief of General Staff). CMC Chairman Jiang Zemin met briefly with Myers, echoing President Bush's brief meeting with General Cao. The PLA generals and Jiang stressed Taiwan as their critical issue. General Myers stressed that the United States has a responsibility under the TRA to assist Taiwan's ability to defend itself and to ensure that there will be no temptation to use force. Myers pointed to the PLA's missile buildup as a threat to Taiwan. The PLA allowed Myers to be the first foreign visitor to tour the Beijing Aerospace Control Center, headquarters of its space program. Myers discussed advancing mil-to-mil contacts, including search and rescue exercises, educational exchanges, ship visits, and senior-level exchanges (including a visit by General Liang Guanglie). Myers also indicated a U.S. expectation of exchanges between younger officers, saying that interactions at the lower level can improve mutual understanding in the longer run.

February 10-11	Under Secretary of Defense for Policy Douglas Feith visited Beijing to hold the 6th DCT with General Xiong Guangkai, a meeting which the PLA side claimed to be "defense consultations at the vice ministerial level." Feith met with General Cao Gangchuan (a CMC Vice Chairman and Defense Minister), who raised extensively the issue of Taiwan and the referendums. Feith said he discussed North Korean nuclear weapons, Taiwan, and maritime safety. He stressed that avoiding a war in the Taiwan Strait was in the interests of both countries and that belligerent rhetoric and the PLA's missile buildup do not help to reduce cross-strait tensions. The PRC's Foreign Ministry said that the two sides discussed a program for mil-to-mil contacts in 2004. The Department of Defense proposed a defense telephone link (DTL), or "hotline," with the PLA.
February 24-28	The USS *Blue Ridge*, the 7th Fleet's command ship, visited Shanghai. In conjunction with the port call, Vice Admiral Robert Willard, Commander of the 7th Fleet, met with Rear Admiral Zhao Guojun, Commander of the East Sea Fleet.
March 9-11	The Maritime and Air Safety Working Group under the MMCA met in Shanghai. The U.S. visitors met with Rear Admiral Zhou Borong, Deputy Chief of Staff of the PLAN, and toured the frigate Lianyungang.
May 3-June 29	A team from the Joint POW/MIA Accounting Command (JPAC) traveled to northeastern city of Dandong near China's border with North Korea on an operation to recover remains of a pilot whose F-86 fighter was shot down during the Korean War. In following up on an initial operation in July 2002 on a Cold War case, the U.S. team also went to northeastern Jilin province to recover remains of two CIA pilots whose C-47 transport plane was shot down in 1952.
July 21-25	PACOM Commander, Admiral Thomas Fargo, visited China and met with General Liu Zhenwu (Guangzhou MR Commander), Foreign Minister Li Zhaoxing, General Liang Guanglie (Chief of General Staff), and General Xiong Guangkai (a Deputy Chief of General Staff), who opposed U.S. arms sales with Taiwan. Fargo said that policy on Taiwan has not changed.
August-September	DPMO sent a team to Tibet to recover wreckage from a site where a C-46 aircraft crashed during World War II.
September 24-27	The USS *Cushing*, a destroyer with the Pacific Fleet, visited Qingdao for a port visit.
October 24-30	Reciprocating General Myers' visit to China, PLA Chief of General Staff, General Liang Guanglie, visited the United States, including the Joint Forces Command and Joint Forces Staff College at Norfolk; the carrier USS *George Washington* and the destroyer USS *Laboon* at Norfolk Naval Base; Air Combat Command at Langley Air Force Base; Joint Task Force-Civil Support at Fort Monroe; Army Infantry Center at Fort Benning; Washington, DC; and Air Force Academy in Colorado Springs. In Washington, General Liang held meetings with National Security Advisor Condoleezza Rice, Secretary of State Colin Powell, and General Richard Myers, Chairman of the Joint Chiefs of Staff. Secretary of Defense Rumsfeld saw General Liang briefly. Talks covered military exchanges, the Six-Party Talks on North Korea, and Taiwan.
November 22-23	DPMO held Technical Talks in Beijing on POW/MIA recovery operations in 2005.

2005

January 30-February 1	Deputy Under Secretary of Defense Richard Lawless visited Beijing to hold a Special Policy Dialogue for the first time, as a forum to discuss policy problems separate from safety concerns under the MMCA. Meeting with Zhang Bangdong, Director of the PLA's Foreign Affairs Office, Lawless tried to negotiate an agreement on military maritime and air safety. He also discussed a program of military contacts in 2005, the U.S. proposal of February 2004 for a "hotline," Taiwan, the DCTs, PLA's buildup, and a possible visit by Secretary Rumsfeld. Lawless also met with General Xiong Guangkai.
February 23-25	Deputy Assistant Secretary of Defense for POW/MIA Affairs Jerry Jennings visited Beijing and Dandong to discuss China's assistance in resolving cases from the Vietnam War and World War II. He also continued to seek access to China's documents related to POW camps that China managed during the Korean War. At Dandong, Jennings announced the recovery of the remains of a U.S. Air Force pilot who was missing-in-action from the Korean War.
April 29-30	General Xiong Guangkai, Deputy Chief of General Staff, visited Washington to hold the 7th DCT with Under Secretary of Defense Douglas Feith. They continued to discuss the U.S. proposal for a "hotline" and an agreement on military maritime and air safety with the PLA and also talked about military exchanges, international security issues, PLA modernization, U.S. military redeployments,

and energy. Xiong also met with Deputy Secretary of Defense Paul Wolfowitz, National Security Advisor Stephen Hadley, and Under Secretary of State Nicholas Burns.

July 7-8	The Department of Defense and the PLA held an annual MMCA meeting in Qingdao, to discuss unresolved maritime and air safety issues under the MMCA.
July 18-22	General Liu Zhenwu, Commander of the PLA's Guangzhou MR, visited Hawaii, as hosted by Admiral William Fallon, the PACOM Commander. Among visits to parts of PACOM, General Liu toured the USS *Chosin*, a Ticonderoga-class cruiser.
September 6-11	Admiral William Fallon, PACOM Commander, visited Beijing, Shanghai, Guangzhou, and Hong Kong at the invitation of General Liu Zhenwu, Guangzhou MR Commander. As Admiral Fallon said he sought to deepen the "exceedingly limited military interaction," he met with high-ranking PLA Generals Guo Boxiong (CMC Vice Chairman) and Liang Guanglie (Chief of General Staff). Fallon discussed military contacts between junior officers; PLA observers at U.S. exercises; exchanges with more transparency and reciprocity; cooperation in disaster relief and control of avian flu; and reducing tensions.
September 13-16	The destroyer USS *Curtis Wilbur* visited Qingdao, hosted by the PLAN's North Sea Fleet.
September 27	U.S. and other foreign military observers (from 24 countries) observed a PLA exercise ("North Sword 2005") at the PLA's Zhurihe training base in Inner Mongolia in the Beijing MR.
October 18-20	Defense Secretary Donald Rumsfeld visited Beijing, China. He met with General Cao Gangchuan (including a visit to the office in the August 1st [Bayi] Building of this CMC Vice Chairman and Defense Minister), General Guo Boxiong (a CMC Vice Chairman), General Jing Zhiyuan (commander of the Second Artillery, or missile corps, in the first foreign visit to its headquarters), and Hu Jintao (CPC General Secretary, CMC Chairman, and PRC president). General Jing introduced the Second Artillery and repeated the PRC's declared "no first use" nuclear weapons policy. Rumsfeld's discussions covered military exchanges; greater transparency from the PLA, including its spending; China's rising global influence; Olympics in Beijing in 2008; and China's manned space program. Rumsfeld also held round-tables at the Central Party School and AMS. The PLA denied a U.S. request to visit its command center in the Western Hills, outside Beijing, and continued to deny agreement on a "hot line." The PLA did not agree to open archives believed to hold documents on American POWs in the Korean War, an issue raised by Assistant Secretary of Defense Peter Rodman and Deputy Under Secretary of Defense Richard Lawless.
November 13-19	The PLA sent its first delegation of younger, mid-ranking brigade and division commanders and commissars to the United States. Led by Major General Zhang Wenda, Deputy Director of the GSD's General Office, they visited units of PACOM in Hawaii and Alaska.
December 8-9	Deputy Under Secretary of Defense Lawless visited Beijing to discuss military exchanges in 2006 and military maritime security. He met with the Director of the PLA's Foreign Affairs Office, Major General Zhang Bangdong, and Deputy Chief of General Staff, General Xiong Guangkai.
December 12-15	A delegation from the PLA's NDU, led by Rear Admiral Yang Yi, Director of the Institute for Strategic Studies, visited Washington (NDU, Pentagon, and State Department).
December 13	Following up on Rumsfeld's visit, a DPMO delegation visited Beijing to continue to seek access to China's archives believed to contain information on American POWs during the Korean War. The delegation also discussed POW/MIA investigations and recovery operations in China in 2006.

2006

January 9-13	PLA GLD delegation representing all MRs visited PACOM (hosted by Col. William Carrington, J1) to discuss personnel management, especially U.S. vs. PLA salaries.
February 27-28	A PACOM military medical delegation visited China.
March 13-18	To reciprocate the PLA's first mid-ranking delegation's visit in November 2005, PACOM's J5 (Director for Strategic Planning and Policy), Rear Admiral Michael Tracy, led a delegation of 20 O-5 and O-6 officers from PACOM's Army, Marines, Navy, and Air Force commands to Beijing, Shanghai, Nanjing, Hangzhou, and Ningbo.

April 9-15	NDU President LTG Michael Dunn and Commandant of the Industrial College of the Armed Forces (ICAF) Major General Frances Wilson visited Be jing, Nanjing, and Shanghai.
May 9-15	PACOM Commander, Admiral William Fallon, visited Beijing, Xian, Hangzhou, and cities close to the border with North Korea, including Shenyang. He met with a CMC Vice Chairman, General Cao Gangchuan, and a Deputy Chief of General Staff, General Ge Zhenfeng, and discussed issues that included the U.S.-Japan alliance and real PLA spending. Fallon was the first U.S. official to visit the 39th Group Army, where he saw a showcase unit (346th regiment). At the 28th Air Division near Hangzhou, he was the first U.S. official to see a new FB-7 fighter. He invited the PLA to observe the U.S. "Valiant Shield" exercise in June near Guam.
May 15-26	The PLA observed Cobra Gold, a multilateral exercise hosted by Thailand and PACOM.
June 8	Assistant Secretary of Defense Peter Rodman visited Beijing for the 8th DCT, the first time at this lower level and without Xiong Guangkai. He talked with Major General Zhang Qinsheng, Assistant Chief of General Staff, about exchanges, weapons nonproliferation, counterterrorism, Olympics, invitation to the Second Artillery commander to visit, etc.
June 16-23	A PLA and civilian delegation of 12, led by Rear Admiral Zhang Leiyu, a PLAN Deputy Chief of Staff and submariner, observed the U.S. "Valiant Shield" exercise that involved three carrier strike groups near Guam. They boarded the USS *Ronald Reagan* and visited Guam's air and naval bases.
June 27-30	USS *Blue Ridge* (7th Fleet's command ship) visited Shanghai.
July 16-22	The highest ranking PLA commander, a Politburo Member, and a CMC Vice Chairman, General Guo Boxiong, visited San Diego (3rd Marine Aircraft Wing and carrier USS *Ronald Reagan*), Washington, and West Point, at Defense Secretary Rumsfeld's invitation. General Guo agreed to hold a combined naval search and rescue exercise (a U.S. proposal for the past two years in the context of the MMCA talks) and to allow U.S. access to PLA archives with information on U.S. POW/MIAs from the Korean War (a U.S. request for many years). Guo personally gave Rumsfeld information on his friend, Lt. j.g. James Deane, a Navy pilot who was shot down by the PLA Air Force in 1956. Guo also had meetings with Representatives Mark Steven Kirk and Rick Larsen (co-chairs of the U.S.-China Working Group), Secretary of State Condoleezza Rice, and National Security Advisor Stephen Hadley, and President Bush briefly dropped by for 10 minutes during the last meeting. During the meetings and an address at the National Defense University, General Guo discussed North Korea's July 4 missile tests, critically citing the U.N. Security Council resolution condemning the tests (remarks not reported by PRC press). In contrast to the meeting in Beijing with General Myers in January 2004, Taiwan was not a heated topic in General Guo's talks with Rumsfeld and the Chairman of the Joint Chiefs of Staff, General Peter Pace.
August 7-11	MMCA plenary and working group meetings held in Hawaii. The two sides established communication protocols, planned communications and maneuver exercises, and scripted the two phases of the planned search and rescue exercise.
August 21-23	PACOM Commander, Admiral Fallon, visited Harbin.
September 6-20	The PLAN destroyer *Qingdao* visited Pearl Harbor (and held the first U.S.-PLA basic exercise in the use of tactical signals with the U.S. Navy destroyer USS *Chung-Hoon*) and San Diego (and held the first bilateral search and rescue exercise (SAREX), under the MMCA, with the destroyer USS *Shoup*).
September 10-21	In the second such visit after 1998, a huge 58-member PLA Air Force delegation, with its own PLAAF aircraft, visited Elmendorf AFB (saw an F-15C fighter) in Alaska, Air Force Academy and Air Force Space Command in Colorado, Maxwell AFB and Air War College in Alabama, Andrews AFB in Maryland, the Pentagon in DC, McGuire AFB and Atlantic City in New Jersey, Philadelphia, and New York.
September 20-30	DPMO Team visited China to discuss POW/MIA concerns.
September 26	USS *Chancellorsville* made a port visit to Qingdao.
September 26-28	Principal Deputy Under Secretary of Defense for Policy, Ryan Henry, visited Beijing and Xian. He briefed PLA General Ge Zhenfeng, Deputy Chief of General Staff, on the QDR of February 2006.

October 8-13   A U.S. delegation from the Office of the Deputy Under Secretary of Defense for Installations and Environment visited China to discuss military environmental issues.

October 20-27   A delegation of NDU operational commanders visited the United States.

On October 26, 2006, a PLAN Song-class diesel electric submarine approached undetected to within five miles of the aircraft carrier USS *Kitty Hawk* near Okinawa. PACOM Commander Admiral Fallon argued that the incident showed the need for military-to-military engagement to avoid escalations of tensions.

October 30-
November 4   PLA mid-level, division and brigade commanders (senior colonels and colonels) visited Honolulu, toured the destroyer USS *Preble* in San Diego, and observed training at Camp Pendleton Marine Base. They were denied requests to have closer looks at an aircraft carrier and Strykers.

November 12-19   Pacific Fleet Commander, Admiral Gary Roughead, visited Beijing, Shanghai, and Zhanjiang, overseeing 2nd phase of bilateral search and rescue exercise (involving the amphibious transport dock USS *Juneau* and destroyer USS *Fitzgerald*), and the first Marine Corps visit to the PRC.

December 7-8   Stemming from the MMCA-related Special Policy Dialogue of 2005, the Deputy Assistant Secretary of Defense held the 1st Defense Policy Coordination Talks (DPCT) in Washington with the director of the PLA's Foreign Affairs Office to discuss a dispute over EEZs.

2007

On January 11, 2007, the PLA conducted its first successful direct-ascent anti-satellite (ASAT) weapons test by launching a missile with a kinetic kill vehicle to destroy a PRC satellite at about 530 miles up in space.

January 28-
February 9   Deputy Chief of General Staff, General Ge Zhenfeng led a PLA delegation to visit PACOM in Honolulu, Washington, Fort Monroe, Fort Benning, and West Point. The U.S. Chief of Staff of the Army (CSA) hosted Ge, who also met with the Deputy Secretary of Defense and Vice Chairman of the Joint Chiefs of Staff in the Pentagon. However, the PLA declined to attend the Pacific Armies' Chiefs' Conference in August and a reciprocal visit by the CSA.

January 30-31   DPMO/JPAC delegation visited China to discuss POW/MIA cooperation.

February 23-28   Commander of Combined Forces Command-Afghanistan, LTG Karl Eikenberry, visited China.

March 22-25   Chairman of the Joint Chiefs of Staff, Marine Corps General Peter Pace, was hosted in China by Chief of General Staff Liang Guanglie and also met with CMC Vice Chairmen Guo Boxiong and Cao Gangchuan. Pace visited Beijing, Shenyang, Anshan, Dalian, and Nanjing, including the Academy of Military Sciences, Shenyang MR (where he was the first U.S. official to sit in a PLAAF Su-27 fighter and a T-99 tank), and the Nanjing MR command center.

April 1-7   PLA Navy Commander Wu Shengli visited Honolulu and Washington, where he met with the PACOM Commander Keating, Pacific Fleet Commander Roughead, Chief of Naval Operations (CNO) Mullen, Deputy Secretary of Defense England, Chairman of the Joint Chiefs of Staff Pace, and Navy Secretary Winter. The CNO, Admiral Michael Mullen, discussed his "1,000-ship navy" maritime security concept with Vice Admiral Wu. He also toured the Naval Academy at Annapolis, the cruiser USS *Lake Erie* in Honolulu, and aircraft carrier USS *Harry Truman* and nuclear attack submarine USS *Montpelier* at Norfolk Naval Base. Wu also went to West Point.

April 15-22   General Counsel of the Defense Department William Haynes II visited Beijing and Shanghai, and met with GPD Director Li Jinai. Haynes sought to understand the rule of law in China.

April 21-28   U.S. mid-level officers' visit to China, led by RAdm Michael Tracy (PACOM J-5). The delegation visited Beijing, Qingdao, Nanjing, and Shenyang, including the East Sea Fleet Headquarters, a Su-27 fighter base, and 179th Brigade.

May 12-16   PACOM Commander Admiral Timothy Keating visited Beijing, meeting with CMC Vice Chairman Guo Boxiong and questioning the ASAT weapon test in January. Keating also met with PLA Navy Commander Wu Shengli and heard interest in acquiring an aircraft carrier. Keating visited the Nanjing MR (including the Nanjing Naval Command, Nanjing Polytechnic Institute, and 179th Brigade). At a press conference in Beijing on May 12, Keating suggested U.S. "help" if China builds aircraft carriers.

June 15-25	In the third such visit and nominally under its Command College, the PLAAF sent a 20-member delegation (U.S. limit reduced from 58 members in September 2006). They visited New York, McGuire AFB (saw KC-135 Stratotanker) in New Jersey, the Pentagon in DC, Maxwell AFB and Air War College in Alabama, Lackland AFB and Randolph AFB (Personnel Center) in Texas, and Los Angeles.
July 23-29	Pacific Air Forces Commander, General Paul Hester, visited Beijing and Nanjing. He met PLAAF Commander Qiao Qingchen and Deputy Chief of General Staff Ge Zhenfeng. Hester visited Jining Air Base (as the first U.S. visitor) and Jianqiao Air Base. He was denied access to the J-10 fighter.
August 17-23	After nomination to be Chairman of Joint Chiefs of Staff, the CNO, Adm. Michael Mullen, visited Lushun, Qingdao, Ningbo, and Dalian Naval Academy. He met with PLAN Commander Wu Shengli and two CMC Vice Chairmen, Generals Guo Boxiong and Cao Gangchuan. After postponing his reciprocal visit (for hosting PLAN Commander Wu Shengli in April) due to inadequate substance and access given by the PLA, Mullen got unprecedented observation of an exercise, boarding a Song-class sub and Luzhou-class destroyer.
November 4-6	Defense Secretary Robert Gates visited China (then South Korea and Japan). Defense Minister Cao Gangchuan finally agreed to the U.S. proposal to set up a defense telephone link (hotline). Gates also sought a dialogue on nuclear policy and broader exchanges beyond the senior level. Gates also met with CMC Vice Chairmen Guo Boxiong and Xu Caihou, and Chairman Hu Jintao.

In November 2007, the PRC MFA disapproved port calls at Hong Kong by U.S. Navy ships, including minesweepers in distress (USS *Patriot* and USS *Guardian*) seeking to refuel in face of an approaching storm, and the aircraft carrier USS *Kitty Hawk* and accompanying vessels planning on a holiday and family reunions for Thanksgiving. On November 28, President Bush raised the problem with the PRC's visiting Foreign Minister, and Deputy Assistant Secretary of Defense David Sedney lodged a demarche with the PLA. When the *Kitty Hawk* left Hong Kong, it transited through the Taiwan Strait, raising PRC objections. In Beijing in January 2008, Admiral Keating asserted that the strait is international water and that PRC permission is not needed for U.S. naval ships to sail in the strait.

December 3	9th DCT was held in Washington. PLA Deputy Chief of General Staff Ma Xiaotian and Under Secretary of Defense for Policy Eric Edelman led discussions that covered PLA objections to U.S. arms sales to Taiwan and U.S. law restricting military contacts, military exchanges in 2008, nuclear proliferation in North Korea and Iran (including the just-issued U.S. National Intelligence Estimate on Iran's nuclear program), lower-ranking exchanges, hotline, PLA's suspension of some visits and port calls in Hong Kong, and U.S. interest in a strategic nuclear dialogue. The PLA delegation included PLAN Deputy Chief of Staff Zhang Leiyu and 2nd Artillery Deputy Chief of Staff Yang Zhiguo. They also met: Deputy Defense Secretary Gordon England, Vice Chairman of the Joint Chiefs of Staff James Cartwright, Deputy National Security Advisor James Jeffrey, and Deputy Secretary of State John Negroponte.

2008

January 13-18	In his 2nd visit as PACOM Commander, Adm. Timothy Keating, visited Beijing, Shanghai, and Guangzhou, before Hong Kong. He visited AMS and Guangzhou MR, and met with PLA Chief of General Staff, General Chen Bingde; CMC Vice Chairman, General Guo Boxiong, who demanded an end to U.S. arms sales to Taiwan. Keating discussed exchanges with a new invitation to the PLA to participate in the Cobra Gold multilateral exercise in May, the PRC's strategic intentions, denied port calls in Hong Kong, etc. (The PLA only observed Cobra Gold in Thailand in May.)
February 23-27	PACOM's Director for Strategic Planning and Policy (J-5), USMC Major General Thomas Conant, and PLAN Deputy Chief of Staff Zhang Leiyu led a plenary meeting under the MMCA in Qingdao, the first since 2006. The U.S. delegation visited the frigate *Luoyang*. The U.S. side opposed PLA proposals to discuss policy differences and plan details of naval exercises at the MMCA meetings.
February 25-29	Deputy Assistant Secretary of Defense for POW/MIA Affairs Charles Ray signed a Memorandum of Understanding in Shanghai on February 29, 2008, gaining indirect access to PLA archives on the Korean War in an effort to resolve decades-old POW/MIA cases.
February 26-29	Deputy Assistant Secretary of Defense David Sedney met with PLA Assistant Chief of General

Staff, Major General Chen Xiaogong, in Beijing. Sedney also led the 2nd meeting of the DPCT in Shanghai. Sedney and Major General Qian Lihua, Director of the PLA's Foreign Affairs Office, signed an agreement to set up a hotline.

Days before Taiwan's presidential election and referendums on March 22, 2008, in a sign of U.S. anxiety about PRC threats to peace and stability, the Defense Department had two aircraft carriers (including the *Kitty Hawk* returning from its base in Japan for decommissioning) positioned east of Taiwan to respond to any PLA provocation or crisis.

March 7-15	PACOM's Deputy Director for Strategic Planning and Policy, Brigadier General Sam Angelella, led a 19-member group of mid-level officers to Beijing, Zhengzhou, and Qingdao.
March 29-April 6	The U.S. Marine Corps Commandant, General James Conway, visited Beijing, as hosted by PLA Navy Commander Wu Shengli. Conway met with Defense Minister Liang Guanglie and spoke at NDU. The PLAN allowed Conway to board an amphibious ship, a destroyer, and an expeditionary fighting vehicle. In meeting Guangzhou MR Commander, LTG Zhang Qinsheng, Conway apparently discussed deploying forces together in disaster relief operations.
April 21-22	The first talks on nuclear weapon strategy and policy held in Washington at the "experts" level.
May 18	After the earthquake in China on May 12, PACOM sent two C-17 transport aircraft from Guam to Chengdu to deliver disaster relief supplies. PACOM Commander Keating used the Pentagon's hotline to discuss that aid with PLA Deputy Chief of General Staff Ma Xiaotian.
June 16-21	Air Force Command Chief Master Sgt James Roy from PACOM led the first U.S. NCO delegation to China. The group of senior NCOs visited the PLA's 179th Infantry Battalion in Nanjing and the Second Artillery (Missile Force) Academy's NCO training school in Wuhan.
July 6-17	PLA LTG Zhang Qinsheng, Guangzhou MR Commander, led a delegation to Hawaii. He met with Admiral Robert Willard, Commander of the Pacific Fleet, at his headquarters and with Rear Adm. Joe Walsh, Submarine Force Commander, during a tour of the attack submarine USS *Santa Fe*. The PLA delegation also observed the RIMPAC exercise. PACOM Commander, Admiral Timothy Keating, agreed with Zhang about planning for two humanitarian aid exercises, the first combined land-based ones, to "push the envelope." The PLA delegation also visited Alaska, Washington, DC, and New York. In Washington, Zhang met with officials of the Marine Corps, Departments of Defense and State, and NSC, including Deputy Secretary of Defense Gordon England.
September 30-October 2	The PLA sent its first "NCO" delegation to PACOM supposedly to reciprocate the U.S. NCO visit in June. However, the PLA delegation was led by Major General Zhong Zhiming, and only 3 out of 13 members in the group were enlisted.
December 17-19	After the PLA suspended some military exchanges in response to notifications to Congress of arms sales to Taiwan on October 3, Deputy Assistant Secretary of Defense David Sedney visited Beijing to try without success to resume exchanges. He met with PLA Assistant Chief of General Staff Chen Xiaogong.

2009

January	The PLA Navy and U.S. Navy coordinated anti-piracy operations off Somalia.
February 27-28	Deputy Assistant Secretary of Defense David Sedney again visited Beijing to resume military exchanges after suspension in October 2008. He held the 3rd DPCT, met with Deputy Chief of General Staff Ma Xiaotian, and then called his meetings "the best set of talks" he has experienced. However, results were limited, and the PLA raised U.S. "obstacles," including arms sales to Taiwan, legal restrictions on military contacts, and reports on PRC Military Power.

On March 4-8, 2009, Y-12 maritime surveillance aircraft, a PLAN frigate, PRC patrol and intelligence collection ships, and trawlers coordinated in increasingly aggressive and dangerous harassment of unarmed U.S. ocean surveillance ships, the USNS Victorious and USNS Impeccable, during routine operations in international waters in the Yellow Sea and South China Sea (75 miles south of Hainan island). The PRC ships risked collision. On March 10, China sent its largest "fishery patrol" ship (converted from a PLAN vessel) to "safeguard sovereignty" in the South China Sea. U.S. press reported the next day that the destroyer USS *Chung-Hoon*, already deployed in the area, provided armed escort to continuing U.S. surveillance operations. On March 10, Director of National Intelligence (DNI) Dennis Blair (also retired admiral and former PACOM commander) testified to the Senate Armed Services Committee that this crisis was the most serious since the EP-3 crisis of 2001, China was being even more aggressive in the South China Sea in the past two years, and there was still a question as to whether China will use its increasingly powerful military "for good or for pushing people around." (For years, China has tried to stake sovereign claims to Exclusive Economic Zones (EEZs) (up to 200 miles from the coast) beyond territorial waters (up to 12 miles from the coast), while the United States and other countries assert access and freedom of navigation in and flight over the high seas.) On March 12, President Obama stressed military dialogue to avoid future incidents to visiting PRC Foreign Minister Yang Jiechi. In May 2009, there was another incident involving the USNS Victorious and PRC fishing ships in the Yellow Sea. In June, the USS *John S. McCain*'s towed sonar array suffered a collision with a PLA submarine off the coast of the Philippines, in what could have been an accident.

April 5-11	Deputy Assistant Secretary of Defense for Prisoner of War/Missing Personnel Affairs (POW/MPA) Charles Ray and JPAC Commander Rear Admiral Donna Crisp visited Beijing and Liaoning province to discuss progress in the PLA's research of archives from the Korean War and toured the PLA's archives.
April 17-21	Admiral Gary Roughead, CNO, visited Beijing and Qingdao in part for the international fleet review for the 60th anniversary of the PLA Navy. Admiral Roughead conducted a working visit with PLAN Commander Admiral Wu Shengli and also met with Defense Minister General Liang Guanglie, and PLAN North Sea Fleet Commander Admiral Tian Zhong. Roughead raised concern about operational safety of naval encounters, port visits and reciprocity, and potential cooperation in anti-piracy and search and rescue.
June 23-24	Under Secretary of Defense for Policy Michele Flournoy visited Beijing for the 10th DCT and met with LTG Ma Xiaotian, Deputy Chief of General Staff. They agreed to hold a special MMCA meeting to discuss disputes over maritime safety and freedom of navigation in the PRC's EEZ. While the U.S. Navy tracked a North Korean ship with suspicious cargo for Burma, Flournoy said they did not discuss enforcement of U.N. sanctions against North Korea and the meeting was not "appropriate" to discuss "operational" matters. They discussed regional security in North Korea, Iran, Afghanistan, and Pakistan. The U.S. side briefed the PLA on the NPR and QDR.
July 27-28	Under Secretary of Defense for Policy Michele Flournoy and PACOM Commander, Admiral Timothy Keating, represented the DOD at the 1st Strategic and Economic Dialogue (S&ED) in Washington, co-chaired by the Secretaries of State and Treasury. Pressed by the U.S. side to participate, the PLA reluctantly dispatched Rear Admiral Guan Youfei, Deputy Director of the Foreign Affairs Office, in charge of mil-to-mil with the United States. The two sides reiterated that they "resumed" mil-to-mil and agreed on visit by a CMC Vice Chairman, General Xu Caihou.
August 19-22	As the first CSA to visit China after 1997, General George Casey visited Beijing and met with Chief of General Staff and Deputy Chief of General Staff, Generals Chen Bingde and Ge Zhenfeng, who complained about U.S.-only "obstacles" in mil-to-mil ties (including arms sales to Taiwan). Casey countered that it was difficult to build a relationship when the PLA's constant starting point was to blame the United States for problems. Still, Casey sought to advance ties and agreed to explore a bilateral humanitarian assistance/disaster relief exercise. Casey also visited the AMS and Shenyang MR and rode in a Type-99 tank. The two sides agreed to "cultural," mid-level officer, and functional exchanges, and humanitarian assistance and disaster relief exercises. General Casey then traveled to Tokyo for the Pacific Army Chiefs conference, which the PLA rejected.
August 26-27	PACOM's Director of Strategic Planning and Policy, Major General (USMC) Randolph Alles, traveled to Beijing for a special meeting under the MMCA. The PLA side complained about U.S. surveillance, while the U.S. side stressed safety as well as freedom of navigation in and over international waters, including the PRC's EEZ.
August 31-September 3	The Director of the Second Department (on intelligence) of the PLA's General Staff Department, Major General Yang Hui, visited Washington and met with the Director of the Defense Intelligence Agency (DIA), LTG Ronald Burgess. Yang also visited the National Defense Intelligence College, National Medical Intelligence Center, and West Point. Yang complained about press reports on the incident in 2006 when a PLAN submarine closely followed the USS *Kitty Hawk* and about alleged terrorist ties of Muslim Uighurs in China's northwest.
September 1-3	The PLA's Archives Department visited Washington, DC, including Gray Research Center at

Marine Corps Base Quantico and National Archives and Records Administration, and met with DPMO to review progress in the first year of the PLA's research on POW/MIAs from the Korean War (as agreed in 2008).

October 24- November 3	A CPC Politburo Member and CMC Vice Chairman, General Xu Caihou, led a 26-member delegation to visit Washington where he publicly presented a propaganda film on the PLA's relief work after an earthquake in China and met with Defense Secretary Robert Gates, National Security Advisor James Jones, Deputy National Security Advisor Thomas Donilon (last meeting at which President Obama dropped by for 10 minutes for a PLA-requested presidential encounter). Gates called Xu his "counterpart" and said both sides agreed to build a "sound and sustainable" mil-to-mil relationship. They agreed to a "7-point consensus" (to exchange senior visits in 2010 by Gates, Chief of General Staff General Chen Bingde, and Chairman of the Joint Chiefs of Staff Admiral Mike Mullen; conduct a maritime search and rescue exercise and other exchanges on humanitarian assistance and disaster relief; cooperate in military medicine; expand service-level exchanges; enhance mid-grade and junior officer exchanges; promote cultural and sports exchanges; and invigorate existing mechanisms for maritime safety). Xu complained about four U.S. "obstacles" to ties (U.S. arms sales to Taiwan, activities in the EEZ off China's coast, the FY2000 NDAA, and DOD reports on the PLA). Gates raised the importance of following up on the nuclear dialogue in April 2008. In the first such PLA visit, Xu briefly visited the Strategic Command (STRATCOM), hosted by General Kevin Chilton. Xu also visited the Naval Academy, Nellis Air Force Base, and Naval Air Station North Island (and the carrier USS *Ronald Reagan*) in San Diego, and visited PACOM, hosted by PACOM Commander, Admiral Robert Willard.
December 16-17	Deputy Assistant Secretary of Defense for East Asia Michael Schiffer held the 4th DPCT in Honolulu with the Director of the Foreign Affairs Office of the Defense Ministry, Major General Qian Lihua. They discussed military exchanges, regional security, and weapon nonproliferation. The U.S. side briefed the PLA on the QDR, and the PLA briefed on its military modernization. Schiffer and Major General Randolph Alles, PACOM J5, sought to reinvigorate the MMCA process to manage problems in maritime and air safety. The PLA proposed to change the MMCA charter, to shift attention away from operational safety to planning for naval exercises and other navy-to-navy contacts.

2010

January 28	After an earthquake in Port-Au-Prince, Haiti, the Army's 82nd Airborne had soldiers conduct the first U.S. combined patrol with U.N. peacekeepers there. The U.N. unit was a PRC paramilitary People's Armed Police (PAP) unit deployed in police uniforms.
April 23-30	Deputy Assistant Secretary of Defense for POW/MIA Personnel Affairs Bob Newberry visited Beijing to discuss accounting for missing personnel.
May 25	PACOM Commander Admiral Robert Willard and Assistant Secretary of Defense Wallace Gregson visited Beijing for the 2nd S&ED and met with Deputy Chief of General Staff, Air Force General Ma Xiaotian and Rear Admiral Guan Youfei, who complained about U.S. "obstacles" (arms sales to Taiwan, U.S. reconnaissance, and FY2000 NDAA). The State Department proposed DOD briefings on the Quadrennial Defense Review and Nuclear Posture Review, but the PLA did not accept the proposal.
September 27-28	Deputy Assistant Secretary of Defense Michael Schiffer visited Beijing to discuss the mil-to-mil relationship with Director of the PLA's Foreign Affairs Office Qian Lihua. The PLA called the meeting merely "working-level" talks and raised concern about U.S.-ROK combined exercises in the Yellow Sea and U.S. policy in the South China Sea. Schiffer also held meetings at the Taiwan Affairs Office (TAO), China Foundation for International Strategic Studies (CFISS), a PLA-affiliated group, and Foreign Ministry.
October 14-15	PACOM hosted an annual plenary meeting of the MMCA in Honolulu. Major General Randolph Alles (USMC), J5, led the U.S. side, but the PLA sent a delegation led only by the PLAN and Rear Admiral Liao Shining, PLAN Deputy Chief of Staff. The U.S. military raised concern about several recent incidents involving unsafe and unprofessional actions by PRC ships as well as aircraft that risked that lives of U.S. sailors and airmen. They agreed to hold future exchanges on maritime search and rescue operations.
December 10	Under Secretary of Defense for Policy Michele Flournoy hosted in Washington General Ma Xiaotian, PLA Deputy Chief of General Staff, for the 11th DCT. Flournoy pointed out the positive tone of the talks with the PLA, which reaffirmed the "7-point consensus" between Secretary

Gates and Xu Caihou in 2009 and the invitation for Gates to visit (January 10-14, 2011), expected right before Hu Jintao's visit later in January. Also, Chief of General Staff General Chen Bingde will visit in 2011. The DCT reviewed discussions under the MMCA, where there remain disagreements over maritime safety and security. They discussed possible cooperation in regional security. The U.S. side briefed on the Nuclear Posture Review, Ballistic Missile Defense Review, and Space Posture Review (the same briefings given to allies), and the PLA briefed on its strategy and modernization. The PLA complained about three U.S. "obstacles" (arms sales to Taiwan, FY2000 NDAA, and reconnaissance in the EEZ off China's coast). Flournoy and Chairman of the Joint Chiefs of Staff Admiral Mike Mullen pressed the PLA side to help end North Korea's provocations and get it to show willingness to denuclearize. (Earlier in December, Mullen publicly criticized China for "tacit approval" of North Korea's belligerence.) Representatives Rick Larsen and Charles Boustany (of the U.S.-China Working Group) hosted a dinner in the Capitol.

December 10   The commander of the PLAN's task force in the Gulf of Aden, also the Director of the PLAN's Navigational Support Department, visited the Headquarters of the U.S. Navy's 5th Fleet at Naval Support Activity (NSA) Bahrain. In return, a U.S. delegation from the 5th Fleet and the Central Command (CENTCOM) visited the PLAN's large landing platform dock (LPD) *Kunlunshan*.

2011

January 9-12   Defense Secretary Robert Gates visited Beijing. The PLA invited Gates to visit in early 2011, though expected in 2010, partly to improve the atmosphere for Hu Jintao's state visit to the White House on January 19. Gates did not travel only to China. He also visited allies Japan and South Korea. Reiterating past proposals, Gates proposed a "sustained and reliable" mil-to-mil relationship, a "strategic dialogue," the 2nd Artillery Commander's visit, and implementation of the "7-point consensus" of 2009 with the PLA. Gates recognized China's helpful role in late 2010 in restraining North Korea, which Gates stressed was becoming a "direct threat" to the United States. The two sides agreed on a new working group to develop a framework for mil-to-mil; combined exercises and other activities in maritime search and rescue, humanitarian assistance and disaster relief, counter-piracy, counterterrorism, etc.; and planning for visits by Admiral Mullen and General Chen Bingde in 2011. Defense Minister Liang Guanglie agreed that a healthy and stable mil-to-mil relationship is an essential part of the positive, cooperative, and comprehensive relationship agreed to by Presidents Obama and Hu, partly to advance "common interests" and to reduce misunderstanding and miscalculation. He agreed on the value of mil-to-mil mechanisms such as the DCT, DPCT, and MMCA, though only to "study" the U.S. proposal of a strategic dialogue (on nuclear weapons, missile defense, space, and cybersecurity) as part of the S&ED. Gates stressed the need to meet under the MMCA to improve operational safety. Gates also met with CMC Vice Chairman and PRC Vice President Xi Jinping, CMC Vice Chairman Xu Caihou, Minister of Foreign Affairs, top leader Hu Jintao, and 2nd Artillery Commander Jing Zhiyuan, whom the U.S. side again invited to visit STRATCOM. Gates asked Hu about the test flight of a J-20 fighter and said that Hu assured that the test was not related to Gates' visit and was surprised by the test.

April 11   Deputy Assistant Secretary of Defense Michael Schiffer visited Beijing for the 5th DPCT and met with the PLA's Director of the Foreign Affairs Office Qian Lihua. However, the PLA referred instead to only a "working-level" meeting.

April 12   Major General Jeffrey Dorko, Deputy Commanding General for Military and International Operations of the U.S. Army Corps of Engineers, visited Beijing and met with PLA Assistant to the Chief of General Staff LTG Chen Yong.

April 26-28   The PLA's Archives Department visited Washington for an annual meeting with DPMO to discuss progress in the PLA's research on POW/MIA cases from the Korean War.

May 9-10   In Washington, the United States and the PRC held the 3rd S&ED. The PLA sent a Deputy Chief of General Staff, General (AF) Ma Xiaotian, the first senior PLA official at the S&ED. The PRC agreed to the first Strategic Security Dialogue (SSD). Stemming somewhat from Secretary Gates' proposal for a Strategic Dialogue, Deputy Secretary of State James Steinberg, Under Secretary of Defense for Policy Michele Flournoy, and Vice Chairman of the Joint Chiefs of Staff General James Cartwright started the new SSD for security talks among military and civilian U.S. and PRC officials. General Ma and Vice Foreign Minister Zhang Zhijun participated together. The initial SSD discussed maritime and cyber disputes. PACOM Commander Admiral Robert Willard also participated in various discussions. Secretary Gates attended the welcoming dinner on May 9, and

Chairman of the Joint Chiefs of Staff Admiral Mullen joined in a luncheon session on May 10.

May 12-21   For the first time, the PLA's band visited the United States (Washington, Philadelphia, New York).

May 15-22   As hosted by Chairman of Joint Chiefs of Staff Mullen, PLA Chief of General Staff, General Chen Bingde, visited along with 2nd Artillery Political Commissar Zhang Haiyang. Chen spoke at NDU, stressing one "obstacle" related to Taiwan and agreement with Mullen on counter-piracy naval exercises. The Joint Staff provided two unclassified briefings. Chen met with Secretary of State Clinton and Secretary of Defense Gates, though not the National Security Advisor. Chen agreed to use the DTL and saw a Predator drone. At Norfolk Naval Base, the PLA had pier-side tours of destroyers and saw simulated landings of carrier-based F-18 fighters. The PLA saw training at Fort Stewart, visited Nellis Air Force Base, and watched urban patrol training in a mock Iraqi village at the National Training Center at Fort Irwin. Chairwoman Ileana Ros-Lehtinen of the House Foreign Affairs Committee criticized the access for the PLA to "sensitive" U.S. military facilities. Members of the House and Senate U.S.-China Working Groups (Representatives Larsen and Boustany, Senators Kirk, Lieberman, and Feinstein) hosted a breakfast for Chen. (In April, Chen hosted a dinner in Beijing for Members of the House Working Group, who toured a PLAN Song-class submarine, the PLA Submarine Academy, and PLA North Sea Fleet Headquarters.)

July 9-13   Chairman of the Joint Chiefs of Staff, Admiral Michael Mullen, visited Beijing, Hangzhou, and Zhoushan Island. He met with General Chen Bingde (Chief of General Staff), General Jing Zhiyuan (2nd Artillery Commander), and Xi Jinping (CMC Vice Chairman and Vice President). Mullen called for exchanges between younger officers and combined exercises (for counter-piracy, medical assistance, and disaster relief). Mullen and Chen discussed disputes over reconnaissance operations, cyber threats, Dalai Lama, Taiwan, South China Sea, and North Korea. Mullen saw a CSS-7 (M-11) short-range ballistic missile at the 2nd Artillery, Su-27 fighter at Jinan MR, counter-terrorist command post exercise of the Nanjing MR, and Yuan-class submarine. Representative Rohrabacher criticized Mullen's efforts as more appropriate for an ally than for a rival.

August 25-26   Navy Captains led the two sides in a Working Group meeting of the MMCA in Qingdao.

September 8   Commander of the Jinan MR, General Fan Changlong, visited PACOM in Honolulu.

December 7   Accompanied by the new director of intelligence (2nd Department) Major General Chen Youyi, PLA Deputy Chief of General Staff, General Ma Xiaotian, hosted Under Secretary of Defense for Policy Michele Flournoy in Beijing for the 12th DCT. Flournoy held constructive talks on regional security in Asia (including U.S. force deployments in Australia, North Korea, Taiwan, Afghanistan, Pakistan, and the South China Sea), the Middle East, and North Africa; agreed to senior visits and exercises in humanitarian assistance and counter-piracy; and assured that the United States does not seek to contain China as an adversary. The PLA merely briefed on its Defense White Paper issued in March and raised "obstacles" to mil-to-mil (blaming U.S. arms sales to Taiwan, FY2000 NDAA, and reconnaissance aircraft and ships). There were no breakthroughs in discussions.

2012

February 14   PRC Vice President, CPC Politburo Standing Committee Member, and CMC Vice Chairman Xi Jinping visited. Like Hu Jintao's visit in 2002, Xi visited the Pentagon. However, unlike Hu's visit, Secretary of Defense Leon Panetta granted Xi a full honors ceremony (including 19-gun salute, national anthems, review of troops, Fife and Drum Corps), in part reciprocating for the reception for Vice President Joe Biden in August 2011. Xi also met with the Chairman of the Joint Chiefs of Staff, General Martin Dempsey. Xi noted that military contacts are important for the U.S.-PRC cooperative partnership. In Congress, 12 Senators (Cornyn, Menendez, Boozman, Wicker, Hoeven, Grassley, Burr, Barrasso, Kyl, Heller, Isakson, and Ayotte) wrote to President Obama on February 10 to urge that he express concerns to Xi about the PLA's modernization, Taiwan, Iran, cyber attacks, intellectual property rights, and human rights. Dempsey testified to Congress on the same day as Xi's visit that the U.S. rebalancing of strategic priorities (so-called "pivot") to the Pacific provides an opportunity to increase engagement with the PLA. Panetta testified on February 15 that talks with Xi covered whether the rebalancing will increase tension with China. Panetta stressed that the United States is a Pacific power and engages from a position of strength.

May 2-4   The Departments of Defense and State held the 2nd SSD during the S&ED in Beijing. Deputy Secretary of State William Burns and Acting Under Secretary of Defense James Miller met with Vice Foreign Minister Zhang Zhijun and PLA Deputy Chief of General Staff Ma Xiaotian to discuss cyber and maritime disputes. Admiral Samuel Locklear III (PACOM Commander), Major General John Davis (Senior Military Advisor to DASD for Cyber Policy), and Brigadier General Terrence

	O'Shaughnessy (Deputy Director for Political-Military Affairs for Asia in the Joint Staff) attended.
May 4-10	As the Defense Minister, General Liang Guanglie visited Washington, DC (meeting with Defense Secretary Leon Panetta, Deputy Secretary of State William Burns, etc.), Naval Base in San Diego, Southern Command, Fort Benning, Camp Lejeune, Seymour Johnson Air Force Base, and West Point. Liang cited "obstacles" of U.S. arms sales to Taiwan, U.S. reconnaissance operations, and FY2000 NDAA. The two sides agreed to combined exercises on HA/DR and counter-piracy.
June 13-14	PACOM and the PLA held a Working Group meeting of the MMCA in Honolulu.
June 25-29	PACOM Commander, Admiral Samuel Locklear III, visited Beijing, Guangzhou, Zhanjiang, and Guilin. He met with Defense Minister General Liang Guanglie, Deputy Chief of General Staff General Ma Xiaotian (host), and GZMR Commander LTG Xu Fenlin. Locklear spoke at AMS. At the South Sea Fleet, Locklear toured a Luyang I-class destroyer at the pier. He led the first military delegation to the GZMR's 121st Infantry Division and rode in a Type 96 tank. The PLA stressed the "obstacle" of U.S. reconnaissance operations and concerns about RIMPAC, U.S.-Japan-ROK trilateral exercises, U.S. "rebalancing" strategy ("pivot" to the Pacific), etc.
August 20-28	Hosted by Vice Chief of the Army, General Lloyd Austin, PLA Deputy Chief of General Staff Cai Yingting visited Fort Hood, Fort Leonard Wood, and the Pentagon. Cai objected to the U.S.-Japan treaty's coverage of the Senkaku Islands. Cai visited U.S. Army, Pacific (USARPAC) in Honolulu.
September 17	In the Gulf of Aden, the U.S. Navy and PLAN held their first bilateral counter-piracy exercise. The USS *Winston Churchill* allowed a visit, board, search, and seizure (VBSS) team from the PLAN frigate *Yi Yang* to conduct a sweep onboard the U.S. Navy destroyer during the exercise.
September 17-20	Defense Secretary Leon Panetta visited Beijing, meeting with Defense Minister Liang Guanglie, and CMC Vice Chairmen Xu Caihou and Xi Jinping. Panetta spoke at the Engineering Academy of Armored Forces. He visited the PLAN's North Sea Fleet in Qingdao and toured a frigate and submarine. He said that the U.S. Navy will invite the PLAN to participate in RIMPAC 2014. He did not reiterate that the U.S.-Japan treaty covers the Senkaku Islands, in three public occasions.
September 27-28	PACOM and PLAN held a plenary meeting of the MMCA in Qingdao. Air Force Major General Michael Keltz (J-5) and Rear Admiral Zhang Jianchang (PLAN Deputy Chief of Staff) led the talks. Keltz also met with Rear Admiral Du Xiping (Deputy Commander of the North Sea Fleet). The two sides discussed differences about the PLA's air intercepts and future mil-to-mil events.
October 10	Rear Admiral Li Ji (Deputy Director of the PLA Foreign Affairs Office) visited Washington for the DPCT with Acting Deputy Assistant Secretary of Defense David Helvey at the Pentagon. PACOM and CENTCOM also participated in discussions about the counter-piracy exercise, maritime safety and security, U.S. rebalancing strategy, cooperative efforts in mil-to-mil plan, etc.
October 27-November 5	U.S. Army Band visited Beijing, Nanjing, and Shanghai, for joint concerts with the PLA band.
November 26-29	Secretary of the Navy Ray Mabus visited Beijing and Ningbo, and saw a frigate, hospital ship, and submarine but not the new aircraft carrier, *Liaoning*, commissioned on September 25.
November 25-December 2	Major General Stephen Lyons, Commander of the 8th Theater Sustainment Command at Fort Shafter, Hawaii, met in Beijing with PLA Deputy Chief of General Staff Qi Jianguo and led about 20 soldiers to Chengdu for a tabletop exercise on cooperation with the PLA in HA/DR.
December 3-7	A PLAN Deputy Commander, Vice Admiral Zhang Yongyi (involved in the aircraft carrier and J-15 programs) visited Pearl Harbor, HI, saw the destroyer USS *Chafee*, and met with Pacific Fleet Commander, Admiral Cecil Haney, and PACOM's Deputy Commander, LTG (USMC) Thomas Conant; visited Washington, DC, and met with Vice CNO Admiral Mark Ferguson (host) and discussed training together at RIMPAC 2014, while CNO Admiral Jonathan Greenert dropped by; visited the Naval Academy at Annapolis, MD; and visited Norfolk, VA, to see Naval Air Station Oceana (saw F/A-18 fighters on display) and Naval Auxiliary Landing Field Fentress (saw practice landings by F/A-18 fighters on airfield) but not Norfolk Naval Base (with aircraft carriers).
December 12	A Deputy Chief of General Staff, LTG Qi Jianguo, visited Washington and met with Under Secretary of Defense for Policy James Miller for the 13th DCT. They discussed maritime security in the East and South China Seas; cyber, space, and nuclear policy; missile defense; North Korea's missile launch; U.S. strategic rebalancing to Asia; Middle East, Afghanistan, and Pakistan.

2013

April 21-25	General Martin Dempsey, Chairman of the Joint Chiefs of Staff, visited Beijing. He met with PRC President and CMC Chairman Xi Jinping, CMC Vice Chairman Fan Changlong, Defense Minister Chang Wanquan, State Councilor Yang Jiechi, and Chief of General Staff Fang Fenghui. General Fang expressed PRC opposition to the DPRK's nuclear tests, but official PRC media left out his criticism. He also opposed cyber attacks for potential effects like those of a nuclear bomb. General Dempsey raised concerns about cyber theft, disruption, and destruction, as well as cyber vulnerabilities in major economies. Dempsey reiterated that U.S. treaty obligations with Japan cover the Senkaku Islands. He explained the strategic rebalancing to the Pacific. He visited the NDU, 4th Helicopter Regiment (saw WZ-9s and WZ-10s), and Army Aviation Academy.
May 6-8	The U.S. Navy and PLAN held a meeting of the working group under the MMCA in Zhanjiang.
May 28-31	Pacific Fleet Commander, Admiral Cecil Haney, visited Beijing and Zhanjiang. Haney met with Deputy Chief of General Staff Qi Jianguo, and CMC Member and PLAN Commander Wu Shengli. Wu asked about U.S. allowing PLA cadets. Haney also oversaw the port visit of the USS *Shiloh*, and visited the PLAN South Sea Fleet's Marine brigade and ships (including the LPD *Changbaishan*).
May 30-June 3	The cruiser USS *Shiloh* stopped for a port visit in Zhanjiang, the first U.S. port visit since 2006.
July 8-12	The Departments of Defense and State, and the PLA and MFA held the 3rd SSD during the 5th S&ED in Washington. Deputy Chief of General Staff Wang Guanzhong led the PLA delegation. Under Secretary of Defense for Policy James Miller, LTG Curtis Scaparrotti (Director, Joint Staff), Brigadier Generals Terrence O'Shaughnessy and David Stilwell (Deputy Director for Political-Military Affairs for Asia), and Admiral Samuel Locklear (PACOM Commander) attended. The Pentagon and PLA agreed on a mechanism to notify about military activities. Defense Secretary Chuck Hagel met with State Councilor Yang Jiechi, and Chairman of the Joint Chiefs of Staff Martin Dempsey met with LTG Wang. As part of the SSD, U.S. and PRC officials held the first meeting of the Cyber Working Group, led by State Department Coordinator for Cyber Issues Christopher Painter and Deputy Assistant Secretary of Defense Eric Rosenbach, and MFA North American and Oceanian Affairs Counselor Dai Bing. U.S. officials raised concerns about cyber-enabled economic theft.
August 16-20	CMC Member and PRC Defense Minister, General Chang Wanquan, visited PACOM in Honolulu; Northern Command (NORTHCOM) and North American Aerospace Defense Command (NORAD) in Colorado Springs; and the Defense Department in Washington, DC. Secretary of Defense Hagel and General Chang announced that PLA Navy midshipmen had started to join a multinational exchange program at the U.S. Naval Academy; the U.S. Joint Staff's J-5 (Strategic Plans and Policy) will start an exchange with the PLA's Strategic Planning Department; the Defense Department is exploring Xi's proposals to President Obama at the summit in June for new Working Groups on notifications of major military activities and standards of behavior for air and naval activities; there will be senior exchanges including the PLA Chief of General Staff's visit in 2014; the two sides will explore support in logistics; and the PLA will deepen cooperation at its archive for research on U.S. POW/MIAs. The day after those remarks, however, the PLA's Director of Foreign Affairs, Rear Admiral Guan Youfei, spoke to selected reporters and sparked a controversy. Guan claimed that Hagel "responded positively" to Chang's proposal to set up a "working group" on U.S. arms sales to Taiwan. However, the Pentagon disputed this claim. The State Department's spokesperson told reporters that there is no change or new announcement, and that the United States makes available to Taiwan defense articles and defense services consistent with U.S. commitments under the Taiwan Relations Act (TRA). Chang also met with National Security Advisor Susan Rice at the White House (not President Obama).
August 19-20	PACOM and the PLAN held a Working Group of the MMCA and discussed HA/DR in Honolulu.
August 22-23	PACOM (J5) and the PLAN held a Plenary meeting of the MMCA in Honolulu. They agreed to set up working groups. The PLA asked to discuss a bilateral "code of conduct" and RIMPAC 2014.
August 24-25	In the Gulf of Aden in the second bilateral exercise on what the U.S. Navy calls counter-piracy operations and what the PLAN calls "escort missions," the destroyer USS *Mason* participated with the PLAN destroyer *Harbin* in cross-deck landing of helicopters on each other's deck and other drills. The U.S. Navy's 5th Fleet talked about sharing "techniques" and increasing "interoperability." The PLA Navy has trained with ship-borne helicopters for "actual combat."

September 6-9	PLAN destroyer *Qingdao* (with Z-9 helicopters), frigate *Linyi*, and supply ship *Hongzehu* paid a port visit to Pearl Harbor, HI. The cruiser USS *Lake Erie* and helicopters held a search and rescue drill with the PLAN on September 9. While the drill did not involve cross-deck landing of helicopters, the U.S. military showed joint operations with an Army Black Hawk and a Navy Sea Hawk. (At PACOM, the U.S. Army has worked with the U.S. Navy in at-sea landing of helicopters.)
September 8-14	Hosted by CNO Admiral Jonathan Greenert, PLAN Commander, Admiral Wu Shengli, visited naval bases at San Diego (including 3rd Fleet that plans RIMPAC), nearby Marine Corps base at Camp Pendleton, and Washington, DC. Wu toured the aircraft carrier USS *Carl Vinson* (in port), nuclear-powered attack submarine USS *Jefferson City* (in port), and littoral combat ship (LCS) USS *Fort Worth* (at sea). Wu's delegation included the commanding officer of the PLAN's first aircraft carrier (*Liaoning*) and the first pilot to complete a tail-hook landing on the carrier. They saw the USS *Carl Vinson*'s combat direction center and arresting gear operations room, and flew in a MV-22 Osprey to Camp Pendleton where they saw static displays of AAV7 and other vehicles.
September 9	Under Secretary of Defense for Policy James Miller held the 14th DCT in Beijing. A Deputy Chief of General Staff, LTG Wang Guanzhong, spoke against U.S. involvement as a "third party" in disputes in the East and South China Seas. They started exchanges on strategic planning. Miller called on the PRC to maintain and increase pressure for the DPRK's denuclearization.
September 24-30	Since the last such visit in 1998, the Chief of Staff of the Air Force (CSAF), General Mark Welsh III, Pacific Air Forces Commander, General Herbert Carlisle, Deputy Under Secretary of the Air Force for International Affairs Heidi Grant, and Chief Master Sergeant of the Air Force James Cody visited Beijing, Nanyuan Air Base, Hangzhou, and Hong Kong. The delegation met with CMC Member and PLAAF Commander Ma Xiaotian, and CMC Vice Chairman Xu Qiliang. The U.S. delegation watched flying exhibitions with J-10s and JH-7s (but did not see J-20 fighters).
November 10-14	Reciprocating PLAN Deputy Commander Zhang Yongyi's visit, Vice CNO, Admiral Mark Ferguson, visited Beijing and Zhoushan. He met with PLAN Commander Wu Shengli and Deputy Commander Xu Hongmeng. Met by Vice Admiral Su Zhiqian, East Sea Fleet's Commander, Ferguson toured destroyer Changchun, corvette Shangrao (at sea), and a Yuan-class submarine.
November 12-19	PLA soldiers held the first field exercise with the U.S. Army. U.S. Army Pacific, Hawaii National Guard, Army Corps of Engineers, and Marine Corps worked with the PLA on tactics, techniques, and procedures concerning HA/DR. The exercise took place at Marine Corps Training Area Bellows on Oahu, HI. The PLA delegation then visited Washington, DC, and Fort Hamilton, NY.
November 18-21	Beijing MR Commander, LTG Zhang Shibo, visited the Pentagon at Washington, DC; Naval Academy at Annapolis, MD; and NORTHCOM at Colorado Springs, CO.

On November 23, 2013, the PRC suddenly announced an "East China Sea Air Defense Identification Zone (ADIZ)," (ECS ADIZ). The "ECS ADIZ" asserted coverage of the airspace over the Senkaku Islands administered by Japan and claimed by the PRC as the Diaoyu Islands and by Taiwan as the Diaoyutai Islands. Moreover, the "ECS ADIZ" overlaps with the existing ADIZs of Japan, ROK, and Taiwan. The PRC Ministry of National Defense issued rules for the "ECS ADIZ" to apply generally to aircraft flying in the "ECS ADIZ" and regardless of whether the aircraft would fly into the PRC's airspace, and threatened actions by the PLA. Secretary Hagel called the development a destabilizing attempt to alter the status quo, stated that the announcement would not change U.S. military operations, and reaffirmed that the U.S.-Japan Mutual Defense Treaty applies to the Senkaku Islands. The U.S. Air Force flew two B-52 bombers from Guam on a long-planned training flight into the "ECS ADIZ" without informing China. On January 23, 2014, Admiral Locklear denied PACOM's surprise by the ADIZ itself, though surprise at how the ADIZ was set up.

December 3	The Cyber Working Group held a second meeting (in Beijing).

On December 5, 2013, a PLA Navy landing ship-tank (LST) almost collided with the cruiser USS *Cowpens*. The PLAN ship ordered and tried to stop the USS *Cowpens* from monitoring the PLAN aircraft carrier *Liaoning* in the South China Sea, after the USS *Cowpens* refused to change its lawful operation in exercising freedom of navigation and leave an area in international waters. The USS *Cowpens* maneuvered to avoid a collision, when the PLAN LST cut in front of the bow of the USS *Cowpens* as close as only 46 yards. Ship-to-ship communication between the captains of the *Cowpens* and the *Liaoning* (who visited in September) helped to defuse the tension. The United States protested to the PRC. On

> December 19, Defense Secretary Hagel called the PLAN ship's action to cut in front of the *Cowpens* "unhelpful," "irresponsible," and "very incendiary." Later, PACOM Commander Locklear said that the near-collision was due to "lack of experience" of the PLA's smaller ships (in remarks to the Surface Navy Association on January 15, 2014).

December 19	U.S. Defense Department officials visited Beijing for a meeting of the DPCT.

2014

January 22-23	Deputy Secretary of State William Burns, Deputy Assistant Secretary of Defense David Helvey, Major General, USMC, Michael Dana (PACOM's J-5), and Brigadier General David Stilwell visited Beijing for the first Interim SSD and met with Deputy Chief of General Staff Wang Guanzhong.
January 21-February 21	PLA soldiers (from the Guangzhou MR) participated in the U.S./Thai-led Cobra Gold exercise (HA/DR only) in Thailand for the first time.
February 21-22	The CSA, General Raymond Odierno, met with Deputy Chief of Staff Wang Ning, Chief of General Staff Fang Fenghui, and CMC Vice Chairman Fan Changlong. They agreed to expand ties between the U.S. Army and PLA ground troops. Odierno visited the Beijing and Shenyang MRs.
April 7-10	Defense Secretary Chuck Hagel visited Qingdao and Beijing. Hagel toured the PLAN's aircraft carrier (*Liaoning*), the first foreign official to do so. Hagel met with Defense Minister Chang Wanquan and CMC Vice Chairman Fan Changlong, who criticized Hagel's remarks perceived as supporting Japan and the Philippines. The two sides agreed to an Asia-Pacific Security Dialogue (covers North Korea's threats) and an Army-to-Army Dialogue. Hagel visited the NDU and Changping NCO School. Hagel invited the PLA to participate in a military medical drill in Hawaii after RIMPAC. Hagel urged the PLA to reciprocate the U.S. briefing on cyber doctrine. Hagel also met with State Councilor Yang Jiechi and Xi Jinping, who cited his agreement with Obama on building the military-to-military relationship. Hagel and Xi discussed North Korea's threats.
May 12-16	CMC Member and Chief of General Staff, General Fang Fenghui, visited San Diego (toured the aircraft carrier USS *Ronald Reagan* and littoral combat ship USS *Coronado* along with PACOM Commander Locklear, observed training by the Marine Corps at Camp Pendleton, and visited a Marine Corps Recruitment Depot); Washington (visited NDU, met with Chairman of the Joint Chiefs of Staff Dempsey, Deputy Defense Secretary Robert Work, Deputy Secretary of State Burns, and Vice President Joe Biden at the White House); Fort Bragg (visited U.S. Army Forces Command); and New York. The two sides agreed to upgrade the DTL to video teleconference. Fang claimed that the PRC oil rig in the South China Sea was 12 nm from Triton Island within the PRC's "territorial waters," but PRC and Vietnamese diplomats placed it at 17 nm from the island.

Author Contact Information

Shirley A. Kan
Specialist in Asian Security Affairs
skan@crs.loc.gov, 7-7606

Acknowledgments

This CRS study was originally written at the request of the House Armed Services Committee in the 108th Congress and is updated and made available for general congressional use.

www.ingramcontent.com/pod-product-compliance
Lightning Source LLC
Chambersburg PA
CBHW080323290526
45790CB00005B/2161